Tucholsky
Wagner
Zola
Scott
Sydow
Fonatne
Freud
Schlegel
Turgenev
Wallace
Twain
Walther von der Vogelweide
Fouqué
Friedrich II. von Preußen
Weber
Freiligrath
Kant
Ernst
Frey
Fechner
Fichte
Weiße Rose
von Fallersleben
Richthofen
Frommel
Hölderlin
Engels
Fielding
Eichendorff
Tacitus
Dumas
Fehrs
Faber
Flaubert
Eliasberg
Ebner Eschenbach
Feuerbach
Maximilian I. von Habsburg
Fock
Zweig
Eliot
Vergil
Ewald
London
Goethe
Elisabeth von Österreich
Mendelssohn
Balzac
Shakespeare
Dostojewski
Ganghofer
Lichtenberg
Rathenau
Doyle
Gjellerup
Trackl
Stevenson
Hambruch
Tolstoi
Lenz
Droste-Hülshoff
Mommsen
Hanrieder
Thoma
von Arnim
Hägele
Hauff
Humboldt
Dach
Verne
Rousseau
Hagen
Hauptmann
Gautier
Reuter
Karrillon
Garschin
Defoe
Baudelaire
Damaschke
Hebbel
Descartes
Hegel
Kussmaul
Herder
Wolfram von Eschenbach
Dickens
Schopenhauer
Bronner
Darwin
Melville
Grimm Jerome
Rilke
George
Campe
Horváth
Aristoteles
Bebel
Proust
Bismarck
Vigny
Voltaire
Federer
Herodot
Barlach
Gengenbach
Heine
Storm
Casanova
Tersteegen
Grillparzer
Georgy
Chamberlain
Lessing
Gilm
Langbein
Gryphius
Brentano
Lafontaine
Strachwitz
Claudius
Schiller
Kralik
Iffland
Sokrates
Katharina II. von Rußland
Bellamy
Schilling
Gerstäcker
Raabe
Gibbon
Tschechow
Löns
Hesse
Hoffmann
Gogol
Wilde
Vulpius
Gleim
Luther
Heym
Hofmannsthal
Morgenstern
Klee
Hölty
Roth
Heyse
Klopstock
Kleist
Goedicke
Luxemburg
Puschkin
Homer
Mörike
La Roche
Horaz
Musil
Machiavelli
Kierkegaard
Kraft
Kraus
Navarra
Aurel
Musset
Nestroy
Marie de France
Lamprecht
Kind
Kirchhoff
Hugo
Moltke
Laotse
Ipsen
Liebknecht
Nietzsche
Nansen
Ringelnatz
Marx
Lassalle
Gorki
Klett
von Ossietzky
May
Leibniz
vom Stein
Lawrence
Irving
Petalozzi
Knigge
Platon
Pückler
Michelangelo
Kafka
Sachs
Poe
Kock
Liebermann
Korolenko
de Sade
Praetorius
Mistral
Zetkin

The publishing house tredition has created the series **TREDITION CLASSICS**. It contains classical literature works from over two thousand years. Most of these titles have been out of print and off the bookstore shelves for decades.

The book series is intended to preserve the cultural legacy and to promote the timeless works of classical literature. As a reader of a **TREDITION CLASSICS** book, the reader supports the mission to save many of the amazing works of world literature from oblivion.

The symbol of **TREDITION CLASSICS** is Johannes Gutenberg (1400 – 1468), the inventor of movable type printing.

With the series, tredition intends to make thousands of international literature classics available in printed format again – worldwide.

All books are available at book retailers worldwide in paperback and in hardcover. For more information please visit: www.tredition.com

tredition was established in 2006 by Sandra Latusseck and Soenke Schulz. Based in Hamburg, Germany, tredition offers publishing solutions to authors and publishing houses, combined with worldwide distribution of printed and digital book content. tredition is uniquely positioned to enable authors and publishing houses to create books on their own terms and without conventional manufacturing risks.

For more information please visit: www.tredition.com

Church Cooperation in Community Life

Paul L. (Paul Leroy) Vogt

Imprint

This book is part of the TREDITION CLASSICS series.

Author: Paul L. (Paul Leroy) Vogt
Cover design: toepferschumann, Berlin (Germany)

Publisher: tredition GmbH, Hamburg (Germany)
ISBN: 978-3-8491-4931-4

www.tredition.com
www.tredition.de

TO
MY FATHER AND MOTHER
WHOSE PUBLIC-SPIRITED AND LIFELONG LOYALTY TO
RELIGIOUS WORK IN A COUNTRY COMMUNITY
HAS BEEN A CONSTANT INSPIRATION
TO CHRISTIAN SERVICE

CONTENTS

PREFACE

Many books have been written during the past few years on the rural church. Some of these have given excellent concrete illustrations of methods that are proving successful in solving local problems. Others have discussed the general rural church situation. The rural life movement, however, has been so rapid that it is believed that a brief restatement of the place of the church in the rural life movement is desirable at the present time.

It has been the task and privilege of the writer for the past four years to be almost constantly in the field traveling from the Atlantic to the Pacific and from Canadian border to the limits of Florida and getting so far as possible first-hand impressions of rural church and community conditions. It is the purpose of the present essay to discuss some of the general problems in rural life presenting themselves to the religious forces of America, and to note some [Pg 8] conclusions as to the next steps to be taken if these forces are to render the service in rural advance that it is believed is theirs to render. Suggestions as to local programs will be made only as evidence that when the church undertakes in an adequate manner the solution of problems whose solution is demanded of it, it receives both the moral and the financial support of the people served. The chapters on phases of the local program are intended only to help in preparing the way for the larger service contemplated.

As with individuals, so it is with institutions. It is difficult to discuss the place of different organizations in the rural life movement without arousing the antagonism of leaders in the respective organizations. It is hoped that the point of view held will be accepted as one of sympathy for the efforts of all organizations concerned and that the purpose of the discussion is to point the way toward a larger cooperation resulting from a better understanding of the work that may be expected of each.

Paul L. Vogt.

[Pg 9]

CHAPTER I

SOME PRELIMINARY DEFINITIONS

When one begins to discuss a subject it helps very much if his readers know what he has in mind in the terms used. In the title selected for this text there are at least three words that need definition. Probably no reader will agree fully with any of the definitions given, but an attempt to define should at least help the reader to understand better in what sense the terms are used by the writer.

The term "community" has come into such common use that it might be assumed that definition is unnecessary. And yet when learned bodies get together to discuss community problems a large part of the time is usually taken up in attempting to define what the different speakers are talking about.

When the writer lived in the open country several years ago he went to Mifflin Center [Pg 10] school and attended Wesley Chapel church. The schoolhouse and the church were located at the same crossroads, and these two institutions drew for their constituency from an area of about four square miles for the school and a somewhat larger area for the church. Brownstown school, to the south, Hendrickson's to the east, and Whetstone to the west made up other school communities. Pleasant Grove church, Salem, and Brownstown, with a different territory covered by each, made up church areas that did not coincide with the school areas bounding Mifflin Center school territory. In like manner, when trading was to be done, Upper Sandusky and Kirby, five and six miles away, were the centers to which everybody went, generally on Saturday afternoon, when friends from other sections of the county might be found on the streets. The boundaries of the trade center were thus much larger than those of either the school or the church. In politics, the center of interest of the particular township with which the writer was concerned was the old schoolhouse turned into a township house at Mifflin Center, the location of the church and [Pg 11] school. The local political interests of the other communities mentioned were at the appointed places in the respective townships. The seat of justice was for some time in the parlor of the writer's father's residence, or in the front yard, to which court was occasionally adjourned when weather conditions permitted. In a larger way county courts were held at the county seat, as were other of the larger political activities.

One could go on indefinitely illustrating the boundaries of interests of various kinds. Some of them centered in the State House; others in the national Capitol; and many a wordy political battle was fought in the little country section over the question as to whether the protective tariff or the Democratic party was responsible for the hard times the farmers and others were suffering. There were even world interests involved, as during the Spanish-American War or the Venezuelan difficulty during Cleveland's administration.

This concrete illustration both raises the question, Which of these is the "community?" and also points the way to the answer. None of the groupings mentioned can be [Pg 12] considered "*the* community." Yet each is "*a* community." A "community" is a psychical and not a physical thing. It can only approximately be bounded by physical lines. In the last analysis the true "community" is nothing more nor less than that group of two or more individuals who are bound together by a single interest. Thus two people living within sight of one another may be members of the same religious community and at the same time be absolutely separated from one another in their political affiliations. Also one person can at the same time belong to many "communities."

But this definition, if adhered to strictly, would lead to confusion of thought perhaps more serious than a less accurate use of the term. Careful investigation of the relation of the different psychic communities to one another reveals the fact that geographically the areas of individual community interest overlap one another; and that in the better organized regions the centers of interests coincide and it is only the boundaries of the several interests that are not coterminous. The Mifflin Center illustration given above is good in that it had the religious, educational [Pg 13] and political interests centered at one physical spot. The social and recreational life of a large part of this local area also was centered here. In the other local groups mentioned there was a division of interest much more marked. A more practical definition, then, of a "community" would be "That aggregation of population which is bound together by a predominating proportion of its local interests."

If this definition is accepted, then an inspection of almost any local aggregation, in the open country at least, will lead to the conclusion that there are few groups of people who have any large number of local interests in common. Perhaps the most powerful force to be considered in determining what is an open country community is that of the social life. People in a given section habitually seek those with whom they are best acquainted when they get together for social affairs of interest outside the family circle; and it is only occasionally that the mass will go out of these habitual associations in seeking social relaxation. This social life may be sought at one time in the school, at another in the church, again at a [Pg 14] picnic, or in the home of some one in the "neighborhood." But the dominating factor is acquaintanceship rather than religion or education or business.

Villages are more easily defined as to the number of interests holding the group together.

One principal objective in the modern local community organization movement seems to be to bring together at some central point the focal points of as many local interests as possible, thus strengthening the community bonds and increasing the community consciousness. As this end is achieved the necessity for the strict definition given above disappears and the "community" becomes *that aggregation of people the majority of whose local interests have a common center.* This is the sense in which the term will be used in this discussion.

The term "rural" likewise conveys a different thought to different people. Indeed, so likely has the term been to mislead that in a recent national survey of religious conditions, the term was abandoned and "town and country" substituted. The simpler plan is to arrive at a definition of the word "rural" [Pg 15] which will include what the latter term connotes. To confuse "rural" with "agricultural" is to ignore both the past and the present in movements of population and in organization of interests. To an increasing degree the interests of the open country are centering in the village, or even larger centers. So that in discussing the problems of the agricultural population it is often necessary to make the center of discussion the organization of the village with an agricultural environment. The better plan is to definitely discuss the problems of the open country under the term "agricultural" and retain the other term for all interests of groups of population in smaller communities, whether in the open country or in the villages. In general, the division of the United States Census will be observed and the term "rural" regularly applied to all groups of under two thousand five hundred population.

At a recent meeting of country ministers an attempt was made to define what is the problem of the rural church. The definition as framed is herewith presented: "The rural task of the church is the nurture and development [Pg 16] of all phases of human welfare in those communities where the general life and thinking of the people are related to matters which pertain to material natural resources."

This definition is inadequate from the administrative point of view in that it would exclude the small manufacturing community, the educational center, the summer and winter resort communities, and similar specialized groups where population is small. The problems of these small communities not directly related to material natural resources have many characteristics in common with those included in the above definition. Size of community has much to do with the type of problem presented; and the one who understands the problems of the agricultural village is probably better able to deal with the problems of the villages of the type mentioned than is the one trained for service in a metropolitan center.

The term "church" is here used in the sense of including all religious forces in rural life. The Sunday School Association, the Christian Associations, Church Federations, and other groups allied to the church are included in the general term.

[Pg 17]

The Manifold Functions of the Church

The church is the only agency in existence that is concerned with man in all his relationships. It is concerned with keeping alive in human consciousness the existence of a Divine Being and of man's relationship to that Being. It is the only agency that proceeds on the theory of the immortality of the human soul and that has a program of preparing the soul for a life after death. In common with other agencies the church is concerned with the individual life of man on this earth and endeavors to lead human beings to that course of life which will result in the maximum of personal spiritual welfare. And in common with other agencies it is concerned with man in his relations to others and to his material environment because these relationships have a vital effect on his spiritual life.

A full analysis of the functions of the church would include a discussion of those features of church work which have to do with man's relation to God and to an immortal existence. But in a discussion of the [Pg 18] church in relation to the community it is not necessary to consider man's relation to God nor to a future life except in so far as beliefs in such relationships influence his personal welfare on this earth or his relationships to his fellow man. Thus this discussion falls in the field of sociology rather than in the field of theology or psychology. A casual observation of the forces at work in human relationships, especially in the smaller communities, leads quickly to the conclusion that beliefs both with reference to God and to a future life have a vital effect on social conduct. But it is the effect instead of the truth of beliefs that is the subject matter to be considered.

Having thus defined the field of our discussion both as to subject matter and as to the phase of the interests of the church to be considered, it is next in order to note the size of the task.

According to the census of 1920, 50,866,899 people in the United States lived in rural territory, that is, in communities of less than 2,500 population. This was 48.1 per cent of the total. For the first time in the history of the country the records showed [Pg 19] a larger proportion of the total population living in urban centers than in villages or in the open country. The population in incorporated villages of less than 2,500 population was 9,864,196, or 9.3 per cent of the total, while that in unincorporated or open country communities was 41,002,703 or 38.8 per cent, as compared with 8.8 per cent and 44.8 per cent respectively in 1910.

The total rural population increase was but 1,518,986, or 3.1 per cent. Incorporated village increase was 1,745,371, or 21.5 per cent, while the unincorporated community population actually decreased 227,355, or .6 per cent.

These figures indicate two conclusions of importance to our discussion. The first is that the villages of less than 2,500 inhabitants are sharing with the large centers in the general increase in population. Their increase proportionately is not so marked as is that of the extremely large centers, but it is sufficiently marked to indicate that they offer opportunities that attract more than does the open country. This village growth must be reckoned with in determining policies of location of church buildings and the [Pg 20] type of local church program for community service.

The second conclusion is that the open country is still at a disadvantage so far as its possibilities of supporting a large population are concerned. Actual depopulation of the open country, the enlargement of the size of farms, the abandonment of acreage once under cultivation, which preliminary figures issued by the Census Bureau indicate, show that not yet is the demand for agricultural products such as to make a much larger open country population possible. This fact also points the direction for readjustment of rural community life.

The data from the religious census of the United States, taken in 1916, while not classified as rural and urban, give hopeful figures as to the progress of religious institutions in this country. While the total population of the United States increased during the decade 1910-20, 14.9 per cent, the church membership from 1906-1916 increased 19.6 per cent. The total church membership increase, 6,858,796, was 50.2 per cent of 13,710,842, the increase in total population. These figures of church [Pg 21] membership increase, covering a period before the European war began to affect this country seriously, indicate that the general rising ethical standards of American life have had their reflection in the larger personal as well as financial support of the religious forces.

While data are not available as to the proportion of rural and urban population belonging to church, the census gives figures as to the church membership in communities of over 25,000 population. According to census estimates, 32.7 per cent of the population lived in cities of over that population in 1916. The religious census shows that 36.5 per cent of the church membership lived in communities of that size. Contrary to popular impression, the larger centers actually have a larger proportionate church membership than do the smaller communities. The facts show that the problem of advance of the Christian Church is more of a small-community problem than it is of the larger centers.

While the proportion of the total population belonging to church increased from 38.1 per cent in 1906 as compared with the 1910 [Pg 22] population to 39.6 per cent in 1916 as compared with the 1920 population, the magnitude of the unfinished task is still almost staggering. If the proportion for rural America were the same as for the country as a whole, there would be 20,143,292 people not belonging to church. Church membership, of course, is not the only criterion of the influence of the church; nor would all denominations admit that all the people should belong to church, since some would not accept children not yet having reached the age of accountability. But in any case Christian America is not Christian even in church membership. This does not take into account matters of social and economic relationships which the spirit of Christianity has not yet penetrated and by which church members as well as nonmembers are bound.

More than 50,000,000 rural folk rising to a consciousness of their inherent solidarity and community of interest, and more than 20,000,000 of these not affiliated with any religious organization, present a challenge for trained leadership unequaled in the history of the world. Urban interests have grown powerful. Urban life has rapidly [Pg 23] advanced for at least the more favored groups until it has far outstripped conditions in rural communities that go to make up the best in modern civilization and culture. Germs have been found in the "Old Oaken Bucket" in the country, while the scourge of typhoid has been banished from the city, and the "Church in the Dell" has crumbled in decay, while the metropolitan pulpit has taken the best leadership for its own. The country has been unable to compete with the urban centers for educational, religious, or social leadership because wealth has accumulated in the cities. Rural population has declined because the prizes in wealth accumulation were in the cities and because it was easier to secure those things there that people have learned to value as most worth while, in good housing, medical attendance, education, and recreation. While city poets have sung the praises of country life, many people who have lived in the country and endured the long hours and little pay from husbandry have, like the Arab, folded their tents and slipped away; and when once they have tasted the advantages of urban life, have not returned.

[Pg 24]

No civilization can be wholesome or permanent so long as any one great group is permanently handicapped in its struggle for economic or social welfare. So long as any group is evidently at a disadvantage the shift of population from the less-favored to the better-favored groups will continue; that is, unless castes are formed which compel people to remain permanently in one group or the other. And this does not happen in modern democratic society. And so long as there is a continuous shift of population in one direction or another we have evidence that conditions are such as to induce the shift.

It is the existence of conditions such as these that makes the challenge for a trained loyal service on the part of those selected to attend to matters concerned with rural public welfare.

It is the purpose of the following pages to outline briefly some of the conditions to which the church must give attention if it is to meet the demand now made upon it by modern rural life. It is not intended to be a treatise on practical theology in the sense ordinarily accepted in courses on that subject. Very little attention will be given to [Pg 25] matters of organization or administration of the local church. It is believed that if only ministers of the gospel can once attain an adequate grasp of the purposes of religious service, the matter of method of accomplishing results may be left largely to the pastors themselves. On the other hand, emphasis upon method, which seems to be demanded by many ministers instead of knowledge of ends to be attained, is more than likely to lead to overorganization, or organization not adapted to objectives. One of the essentials in all leadership is that of having definite objectives toward which to work, and it is the purpose of this text to call the attention to objectives and to organization, both local and general, adapted to the attainment of objectives rather than the methods of attaining them.

[Pg 26]

CHAPTER II

THE BASIS FOR COMMUNITY SERVICE

The past few years have witnessed a marked widening of the concept of the functioning of the church. But there is still considerable question concerning the basis for the program of church work that now bids fair to become conventional. Not long ago the writer attended a convention of a state social welfare association. Over three hundred and fifty persons were in attendance representing the leading agencies for the advance of social welfare in the entire commonwealth, both urban and rural. Careful inquiry revealed the fact that but one minister had registered, and he was on the program. On the other hand, it is the rare occurrence for those professionally interested in social service to be present at a convention of representatives of religious orders. In practice there is still a clean-cut dividing line between those interested in social progress [Pg 27] and those engaged in so-called religious work. The social workers are not irreligious; many of them believe their service to be of the highest type of religious expression. The representatives of the church are welcomed by social workers into their councils, but it is feared that often these representatives are not taken seriously because for so long they have had a program that affected social welfare in but an indirect way. The time has come when representatives of the church should accept their rightful position as leaders in all movements that tend to make human existence more Christ-like and to make the kingdom of heaven on earth more of a reality.

The reason for the attitude of both ministers and people toward the church has been the emphasis placed upon individual regeneration as the sole and all-important method of advancing the Kingdom. The "conversion" of the individual would lead him into right conduct. When all individuals were converted then the kingdom of heaven would indeed be at hand.

But the advance of social science has made clear the fact that the individual is very [Pg 28] largely the expression of the group in which he lives. Custom, convention, fashion, public opinion, and other group influences go far to determine what individual thought and action will be in any given group. The Tennessee mountaineer has a different standard of what constitutes true religion from that of the New England Unitarian. The code of race relationships in Mississippi is not the same as that in Wisconsin. The standards of the boy's "gang" determine largely the dress, the ideals, and habits not only of youth but of the coming man. Even in the life of the individual different standards exist suitable to the several groups in which he carries on his habitual activities. The capitalist who corrupts Legislatures with impunity in business or who prevents child-labor legislation may be a model Christian gentleman in his home and church life.

It is admitted that in the last analysis the group mind can have its existence only in the individual minds that compose it. But it is also true that when we consider the minds of individuals working in groups with the consciousness of what the reactions of others are, the results are different from what they [Pg 29] are when the individual acts alone. Moreover, individuals as a class react in much the same way to stimuli that affect all of the members of the group at a given time. If the price of milk is raised so that there is suspicion of profiteering, common resentment appears. If the leadership of a political party is threatened, the politician, even though he loses leadership, rarely bolts his group. Instead he finds some excuse for standing by the party organization. It is not necessary to alter the minds of all individuals by "conversion" in the conventional manner either to change public opinion, alter physical conditions, or change the form of social organization. When these changes are effected in the minds of the controlling elements of the group, then the entire public mind and social organization are altered and the social process goes on stimulated in newer and, it is hoped, better directions.

One or two illustrations should make this point clearer. Several years ago it was the custom to use common drinking cups on railways. When first legislation was passed to prevent such use, considerable public opinion opposed it as foolish. Now, it is difficult [Pg 30] to get any one to touch a common drinking cup even in the home. Before the elimination of the saloon powerful and sometimes very respectable forces were lined up in favor of its continuance. But as soon as the fight against the saloon had been carried to the point of its legal elimination many of those who once supported the barroom because of the profit to them became its opponents. Formerly the saloon was a center for the corruption of many if not most of the youth in the community. Now, most communities are bringing up a far higher grade of young people morally than they once were because it is no longer necessary to fight against this center of immoral infection.

The lesson these illustrations should teach is this: that the conventional method used by the churches during the past half century of depending almost entirely upon individual regeneration through personal appeal as a means of salvation of the race has handicapped the church and limited its effectiveness. When it is once understood that the mind and the character of the individual can be influenced in as many ways as there are [Pg 31] social contacts, and when the means of approach through all these contacts is understood, then the effectiveness of the church will be immeasurably increased. Social life must be saved not only through individual regeneration but also through the establishment of a right attitude on the part of the individual and as many individuals as possible. On the other hand, individual attitudes can be established in large part by bringing about, through means now fairly well understood, good economic conditions and social organization.

The sad part about the traditional limited method of approach to improvement of group life has been that in probably the majority of cases impulses were aroused by personal appeal to do good and then through ignorance of objectives in group advance those impulses were allowed to die. The "backslider" is an excellent illustration of the results of periodic renewal of impulse to right living. In most other cases the impulses thus aroused have found their expression in a hypersensitiveness in regard to certain phases of personal conduct. Emphasis upon personal moral conduct to the exclusion [Pg 32] of effective interest in social progress characterized much of the product of the personal evangelistic campaigns carried on periodically during the past two or three generations, while the real work of making the world better has been directed by men and women not particularly subject to these periodical waves of religious impulses but imbued with a steady abiding faith in the worth of social action. They have had the good impulses, but these impulses have been steadied and rendered permanently valuable because faith based on knowledge of objectives was available.

If the serious errors of the past are to be avoided it will be necessary for those intrusted with responsibilities of church leadership to vastly increase their knowledge of problems of group life and of methods of control of group life. The following pages are designed to aid the prospective religious leader, either professional or lay, as far as possible in understanding some of the problems that must be dealt with in making human life what Christianity hopes for. Results already have been achieved sufficient to place beyond question the principle that the [Pg 33] church must approach life from every possible angle. The effort to produce right attitudes in the individual must be continued, but the methods used must be varied and multiplied.

Furthermore, before the sound point of view with reference to the method of approach to the problems of the church can be obtained it will be necessary to have a clear understanding as to the place of the child in the moral order. Those who derive their theology by reading and interpreting isolated passages of the Scriptures sometimes arrive at unexpected, and, from the point of view of rational living, eccentric and positively harmful conclusions. Some devoted readers find in the writings of Paul something about "Whereas in Adam all die, in Christ all are made alive"; and in Christ's words the utterance to Nicodemus, "Except a man be born again he shall not enter the kingdom of heaven." They have drawn from these doctrines that all men are born with sin inherent in their natures and that there is no good in the soul until "conversion" has taken place. So long as these doctrines find a place in the preaching and practice [Pg 34] of churches the method of world salvation will be radically different from that for which the writer is contending.

In brief, if the words of Christ are taken at their face value when he said "Suffer little children to come unto me, for of such is the kingdom of heaven," we have an entirely different basis of approach to our problem than if we assume that all are lost except those upon whom the mystical influence of "conversion" in the traditional sense has operated. If the assumption that children are born good is accepted, then we are brought to the question, "How may these innocents be kept so?" The answer is, By training them to control their natural impulses, good in themselves but likely to lead into wrong if not properly directed; and by cultivating the natural tendencies to good that find expression in every normal child. They must also be brought to an understanding of what Christ means to them as their Saviour and Guide. Then this must be supplemented as rapidly as possible by the organization of group life, in such a way that evil influences will be eliminated.

The saloon was not many years ago the [Pg 35] center of corruption of thousands—yes, millions—of the growing youth of this country. The elimination of the saloon has made possible the development of millions of young people free from the particular type of sinfulness for which the saloon was responsible. In like manner, the elimination of commercialized vice has rendered our cities incomparably safer for our young men and women than they once were. The substitution of wholesome amusement for young folks in good environment for the unregulated commercialized amusements once the sole source of recreation has exerted a moral influence too far-reaching to be estimated. The introduction of cooperation in industry has eliminated the sin accompanying the fights between capital and labor in those industries where it has been introduced. These illustrations show how it is possible, by continuing the improvement of social and economic conditions to create such an environment as will destroy the sources of individual corruption and degeneration and will make the growth of the child a continuous succession of stages of spiritual improvement and growth. "Conversion" can thus conceivably [Pg 36] become a conscious personal acceptance of Christ and of the principles of Christianity as the normal basis for right living without a noticeable break in the course or direction of life rather than the intense emotional cataclysm that so often characterized the change in hardened sinners.

When children good by nature are brought up in an environment physical and spiritual that has been brought into harmony with the laws of God, then the problems of evil will be reduced to those arising out of natural causes over which man has not achieved control; and children will be looked upon as the natural and rightful members of the church instead of being kept out of the church until they reach the age of accountability. The burden of getting out of the church should be put on the child instead of the usual responsibility of deciding to come into it.

It is customary for leaders of the church to assume credit for practically all the good things going on in the direction of human improvement by assuming that, though the church does not have a large membership, comparatively speaking, its influence has [Pg 37] inspired the good work being done in social progress. It is well to face frankly the fact that, whatever may have been the situation in the past, at the present it is questionable whether the church has been the source of even the larger portion of this inspiration. The public schools, including the higher institutions of learning, have been socializing the future leaders in social progress so that their inspiration has been drawn from a concrete knowledge of social problems and from the belief that humanity can, by proper effort, control conditions of living. Then pragmatic results have furthered this belief until inspiration has come from the achievement of results themselves rather than from any recognition of Christian influence in social life. The Christian religion is doubtless responsible for those things most worth while in modern life, but other sources of inspiration have developed for which Christianity does not get the credit.

The conclusion of the whole matter is that in the past two or three generations two marked divisions have grown up, the one a section or wing inside the church which has placed sole emphasis upon individual regeneration [Pg 38] as the method of social progress; the other largely outside the church, with emphasis upon social reform as the method of advance. What is needed is a widening of the field so that the methods of social improvement proved to be of value by social workers will be adopted as valid methods of bringing about the kingdom of God. On the other hand, social workers must give more attention to the regeneration of the individual. When each of these groups recognizes the value of the program of the other, then it will be difficult to distinguish longer between churchmen and social workers. The two groups will, in fact, join hands, and by unifying and coordinating efforts will work more effectively in attaining a common aim. The basis, then, for the program for the church which will touch all phases of human interest in a vital way is that every human interest has its effect on the welfare of the soul. And a program that fails to take into account every approach to the individual can at least be but partial.

Again, it will be necessary to revise popular impression as to just what is spiritual. The farmer who after having a most unusual [Pg 39] "spiritual experience" at a revival service angrily opposed a local movement for consolidation of schools because such a move would increase taxes had an idea of religion that was strictly personal—and anti-social. The church leader who feared that the encouragement of social-center activities by the church would ultimately result in a condition in which the social activities of the church would overshadow the "spiritual," had in mind a distinction that must be met and understood if the church is to broaden its program without losing its identity as a religious institution. The minister who, while praising a community-club movement which had brought to the community many improvements and a better moral condition, stated that it was injuring the "church," either saw a real conflict between "spiritual" and "social" welfare or had a misconception as to what is spiritual.

The problem seems to arise out of a tendency which has crept into theological thought to limit "spiritual" things to mystical personal experiences. With this definition of spiritual things there seems to have come a tendency to look upon any type of [Pg 40] activity that was of a practical nature, such as providing for the recreational needs of the community, organizing a campaign for better reading facilities for country people, or for better farming, as not spiritual, and consequently be sedulously avoided by the church. Perhaps there is no thought in American rural life to-day that causes more trouble to the aggressive rural minister of the modern type than this. His young men and women want to broaden the scope of the church, but the trustees, and those whose word counts toward the selection of pastors and their removal, often oppose anything being done by the church which is not customary and accordingly, as they think, not spiritual.

Christ said "I am come that ye might have life, and have it more abundantly." If this statement is accepted at its face value, then we have the foundation for judging every activity in which the church may partake. Does the activity tend to increase the material and spiritual welfare of the community, so that the influences that tend to the extermination of the group are less? If so, then it conforms to the purposes of the [Pg 41] coming of the Christ. On the other hand, if the activity does positively lessen the resistance of the community, reducing it ultimately to a lower scale of living characterized by those things that are recognized as harmful, then it is not a legitimate part of church work. It also follows that if such harmful conditions exist in the community without a protest on the part of the church or without some definite effort to eliminate them, then the church is not living up to the high calling expected of it by the Master. The term "spiritual" is, accordingly, much more inclusive than has been popularly supposed, and one of the great contributions of social science during the past few decades has been to bring to the public mind the knowledge that man and his spirituality cannot be dealt with individually but must be included in all those relationships that affect the soul of the individual.

While the succeeding pages have to do with the social aspects of the spiritual life of man, it must never be forgotten that the regeneration or the quickening of the individual is at least half of the task in community progress. The life of the honest, upright [Pg 42] man, whose soul has been set on fire by contact with the flame of divine love, whose heart has been brought into harmony with the divine will of God, becomes in itself a point for the radiation of impulses for right living. And when these impulses are directed into useful channels through a broadened understanding of sound objectives in social progress, then real advance is possible.

There are many other phases of thought that act as a hindrance to the advance of the spiritual kingdom in rural America, but these illustrations will be sufficient to show what must be cleared away before the broad program of the modern rural church can be wholeheartedly accepted. In fairness to the writer it should be kept in mind, as stated in the definitions given at the opening, that this text has nothing to do with those vital elements of religious organization and service which are intended to keep alive man's belief in a divinity and in immortality except in so far as these beliefs affect community relationships. The discussion of these subjects falls, rather, into the realm of theology. It is hoped that at least the [Pg 43] principles underlying the movement toward broadening the program of the rural church have been clearly, if briefly, stated, and that the movement toward a larger concept of the religious forces as a factor in rural progress will continue to spread at an accelerating speed.

28

[Pg 44]

CHAPTER III

THE ECONOMIC CHALLENGE TO THE CHURCH

As one travels through the rural districts of America and observes differences in the standards of living he is convinced that human welfare depends very largely on economic conditions. The broad, well-tilled fields of Iowa, surrounding large, well-built houses, big red barns and other outbuildings, form a marked contrast with the patches of corn in irregular fields cleared from the brush and scrub trees on hillsides in Tennessee or Kentucky, and the hovels and rundown farm buildings which go under the name of homes for the hill people. Healthy, well-dressed, happy children attending good schools of the most modern type in the corn belt undoubtedly have the advantage of the boys and girls in the hills who often do not learn to read and write before they are ten years old, if at all, and when they do go to school must be taught by poorly trained [Pg 45] teachers for short terms, ending before the holidays, and in one-room schools often attended by nearly a hundred children. Religious service and leadership in the one section under the direction of college and theological seminary men can hardly be put in the same class with the highly emotional expression of religious impulses of the mountain section led by once-a-month absentee pastors with no education, or, worse still, by wandering so-called evangelists of doubtful morality. One could go through the whole list of contrasts between the economically well-favored sections of the country and the less favored agricultural sections and in no way would the advantage be on the side of the latter.

Efficient social and religious institutions cannot be built on poor economic foundations. So long as a section of the country cannot afford to pay more than five hundred dollars per year for teachers or preachers, it cannot hope to have the leadership possible to another section where ministers to rural people can easily secure eighteen hundred to three thousand dollars per year. Good buildings cannot be erected, nor can any of the [Pg 46] material comforts which go to make up the foundation of civilized life be enjoyed.

For the sake of the church, as well as the people, the church must attend to the economic foundations of rural life. It is unfortunate for many parts of the United States that the ministry has become so separated from real life by the mystical trend in religion that it has rendered practically no service in laying the foundations for the continuance of the communities themselves.

The shift of population from rural to urban centers which the census records show has continued, if anything, at an accelerated speed, indicates the seriousness of the problem. A part of the shift is doubtless due to improvements made in methods of production. So far as this is the cause there is no reason to be disturbed over the tendency, as it is useless to try to keep young men and women in an occupation that does not offer opportunity for earning a living. Part of the shift may be due to the living conditions in the country. This is but an indication of the task of the church on the social side and can be changed as economic welfare permits. But the fact that rural population has been [Pg 47] leaving the farms and that agricultural lands have been abandoned by thousands of acres, indicates that urban opportunities have far outbid the rural in financial returns, variety of openings, and in working conditions. The farmer's income must be increased as compared with other groups before there can be a well-balanced relatively stable American life. Until this is achieved those who are trying to build up rural institutions as strong as those in urban centers will be engaged in a hopeless task.

Eminent, conscientious Christian gentlemen, leaders in religious thought, and occasionally country ministers, have accused those who maintain that the church should have a vital active interest in improving economic welfare of trying to make hog-cholera experts out of preachers, thus taking them away from their real tasks. It is believed that knowledge of hog cholera and of the agencies that can help the farmer to prevent it will not injure the standing of any rural minister. It is maintained with reference to care for economic welfare that it is the business of the church to encourage economic improvement so far as possible (1) by giving [Pg 48] advice and assisting in demonstration work when no other organized agency is in a position to render this service, and (2) by opening the way to other organized agencies to perform this service. This is the prime business of the agricultural colleges through their extension service. But it has been the experience of agricultural colleges that they have the greatest difficulty in establishing relationships in those agricultural sections where their service is needed the most. The minister of the gospel, being one of the two or three paid leaders in a local community, enjoying a measure of the confidence of the people, and having a large part of his time available for pastoral duties, has the opportunity and the obligation to tactfully bring to the community the assistance of these other agencies now provided by the State. When he has done this he can rest assured that he has accomplished something that will become the foundation for a far higher, more satisfying rural life.

Although ultimately the problem of production in agriculture will probably be a most serious one, because of influences such as soil-mining, deforestation, and depletion [Pg 49] of soil through erosion, the immediate problems are, rather, the adjustment of production to demand so that the farmer will be on a more equitable income basis with other elements in the population. When there is newspaper talk of again burning corn for fuel, when wool is a drug on the market, and when farmers' organizations are urging the decrease in the acreage of cotton, it is idle to talk of agricultural welfare being synonymous with ability to increase crop acreage or production per acre. Agricultural colleges and other State agencies have devoted the large part of their efforts to study of problems of production. The results of their services to date have been to so improve production as to hasten the population movement from the farms to the cities. This tendency to aid production to the point of exceeding equitable demand has been of economic value to the great centers but it has not encouraged the continuance on the farm of a large population, nor has it enabled the farmer to compete with the townsman in maintaining a satisfactory standard of living. It would seem that the producing ability of the farmer has been his misfortune, [Pg 50] and that his friends who have taught him to produce more have been his worst enemies.

When a manufacturing plant closes down because it cannot sell its goods at a given price, or when a retailer refuses to handle goods below a price believed by many to be excessive, little is said. But when the farmer tries to adjust his production to demand by limiting production there is widespread criticism of his conduct. There should be continuance of efforts to retain the fertility of the soil, to improve methods of cultivation, and to prevent destruction of wide areas through erosion. The patrimony of the nation must be preserved through wise policies of reforestation and reclamation of waste lands. But the great immediate task is that of adjusting production to demand so that the rural population may advance in material welfare along with other groups. In a competitive organization of industry the farmers success is gauged by his net income rather than by the number of bushels of corn or bales of cotton he produces.

A sinister tendency in the higher-priced general agricultural sections is that of [Pg 51] increase in the number of farms operated by farm tenants. Certain writers have attempted to prove that this tendency is taken too seriously. But the evidence of the United States Census from decade to decade indicates that the danger is real; and that the sooner a policy of control is adopted the better.

The handicaps to agriculture through this increase are manifold. In a large proportion of cases, as shown by studies in typical areas, the landowner does not live on a neighboring farm, nor is he a retired parent or other relative of the tenant farmer. He lives in the neighboring city. Consequently, the rental from the farm goes to help build up the material welfare of the urban center. The contributions of the absentee landlord to church work go to supplement the salary of a city pastor on a scale far beyond the competing ability of the rural church where his land is located. His contributions to benevolences are paid for out of the income from his four-hundred-acre farm but are credited to the city church of which he is a member instead of to the rural church in the community where his land is located. [Pg 52] Because of the transient nature of his residence the tenant, who remains on the farm on the average less than two years, has but little permanent interest in the life of the community and lacks the stability to become a valuable factor in building up strong rural institutions. The landlord, as previously suggested, has been known to oppose measures for consolidation of rural schools because such consolidation might increase taxes, and has been known to threaten tenants with dispossession if they should vote for consolidation. The constant moving of the tenant has handicapped the children in getting a good common-school education because of the breaks in their training resulting from this constant changing of residence.

The tenant house, with all its implications of class-distinction, has come to the country side in increasing numbers. And slowly but gradually a landed aristocracy is growing up in rural America as marked as the landed aristocracy based on the purchase of a few acres of Manhattan Island several generations ago. And with the tenant has come the farm laborer, alien to the community, transient, and as much a [Pg 53] member of the proletariat as if he were working in a great factory in the city. The I. W. W. movement in the wheat fields and lumber camps of the Northwest is but the beginning of the wage-earning consciousness as it spreads out from urban centers.

The short term of tenant operation is lowering the standards of agriculture. Instead of farming on a long-time schedule, expecting returns on a system of husbandry reaching through the years, the tenant is inclined to produce such crops as can be disposed of at the close of the year, regardless of the effect of such a form of agriculture upon the fertility of the soil. Tenant contracts as yet offer little inducement for the tenant to remain permanently on a given farm or to keep up needed improvements.

The tenant for the time being may even make larger profits as a tenant than as an owner. But the tendency everywhere for rents to rise, and the consequent increase in the value of the land, will ultimately bring the tenant to the position of securing from his labor on the farm an income not much in excess of what he would receive from working as a day laborer. The result in the long [Pg 54] run will be that the best agricultural sections of the country will be occupied by a population lower in ability than in a landowning section and constantly kept down by poverty. This prediction may be deemed fanciful by some, but the writer believes that it is worthy of the most careful consideration and study.

Since the organization of the great combinations in the oil and sugar industries during the 70's and 80's of the past century the movement toward close industrial organization has proceeded with little interruption. Legislation has been passed designed to break up industrial combinations and from time to time various industries have been disintegrated. But the layman has not been able to discover that such disintegrations by court order have had any marked influence on the progress of the fundamental tendencies toward industrial consolidation. The farmers have been the last to get into the organization field on any extensive scale. The Grange and the Farmers' Alliance, and later the Farmers' Union, have made attempts and, although many failures are recorded, their work paved the way for a far [Pg 55] larger movement toward farm organization now under way. The tendency toward close organization of industrial groups may also be seen in the labor movement, the American Federation of Labor and the Industrial Workers of the World in this country, and the syndicalist movement in Europe; and in the organization of employers' associations and the National Chamber of Commerce on the part of business men. Whatever may be thought of the unfortunate phases of this movement toward closely organized group consciousness, however Bolshevistic it may be said to be, it must be recognized that class consciousness has come to stay. The old-type citizen who voted as a Republican or a Democrat and as an individual regardless of his industrial affiliations is passing away, and to-day the business men as a class, the wage-earners as a class, the farmers as a class, approach the leaders of both traditional parties with their ultimatums as to what they will do if certain policies are not recorded in their respective platforms. And the best-organized groups, those that can swing the most votes or can produce the largest financial inducements, are the ones that get most [Pg 56] consideration. This may be Bolshevism, but if it is, it is a fact in American life, and we may as well adjust ourselves to handling the situation wisely instead of lamenting the passing of the system of individual representation which was the basis on which American government was founded.

The farmer cannot be accused of leadership in this change in the American State. Business men and wage-earners began it, and the farmer has been forced to follow their example. The old type individualism of the landowning-operating farmer has long handicapped the farmer in his relations with other industrial groups. And it is with many mistakes and setbacks that he is now endeavoring to follow the example so ably set by the multimillionaires of the other groups. Better organization, not for exploitation but for protection and maintenance of a safe balance of influence in economic affairs, is fully justified, and the minister of the gospel is serving the farmer best when he encourages right and efficient organization.

The American Farm Bureau Federation, begun a few years ago through the encouragement [Pg 57] of county agricultural agents in order to give them a point of contact with groups of farmers and to give local support of the county agent's work, has now taken into its own hands the task of farmer organization. And now, with re-sources far beyond what could have been dreamed of a few years ago, this organization is embarking on programs of farmers' business organization almost too staggering in their size to be compre-hended. If rightly managed, and if farmers can prove loyal to their own organization, this movement is destined to solve many of the problems of intergroup relationships confronting the farmers during the past few decades.

As a part of the modern farmer organization' movement, and holding within itself the largest promise of social values, is the encouragement of cooperation. Since the days in 1844, when a little group of wage-earners in England, out of work and gathered round a fire in a tavern, decided to go into business for themselves on a basis of one-man one vote, and distribution of profits on business done with the concern instead of stock held, the movement has continued to [Pg 58] spread all over the world until to-day it holds a very important place in many lines of industry in leading countries.

In this country cooperation has been an agricultural rather than an urban development, primarily because economic conditions have made it more necessary in agriculture than elsewhere. Farmers' elevators, live-stock shipping associations, insurance companies, fruit-and produce-marketing organizations have all gained a sound footing and each year shows an increase in their numbers. The movement has been consistently fought by competitive profit-seeking interests but without avail further than to delay the movement. In the early days discrimination in furnishing cars, underbidding, misrepresentation, adverse legislation all had to be overcome, in addition to the fact that ignorance of business principles often led to failure. Even now, within the past five years, agricultural colleges have been prevented from adding advisers on cooperative organization to their extension staffs, retail merchants' associations have prevented cooperative organization legislation, and insidious attempts have been made [Pg 59] to prevent popular education with reference to the movement.

The cooperative movement offers the greatest opportunity for the country minister for definite service in the farmers' economic progress. The principle underlying the movement is "Each for all, and all for each." Instead of the capitalist and laborer being in opposite camps under the necessity for bargaining, and each doing as little as possible and getting as much as possible for their respective shares of the product of the industry, the cooperative movement brings them into harmony for production of goods, in the belief that all are to share fairly in what is produced. The storekeeper and the buyer no longer haggle over the price because both will share in the returns of the business done. The cooperative movement bids fair to solve many of the problems of open and closed shop, collective bargaining, labor organization, and of relations between producer and consumer. Its steady growth is bringing about industrial peace and since it represents the true spirit of Christianity the minister is justified in encouraging its development wherever he may be.

[Pg 60]

What is the challenge to the church of the economic conditions and tendencies outlined above? First and foremost, the minister must in season and out of season preach honesty in business relations. One of the most important discoveries in the study of problems of the farmer's business relations is that his success or failure depends largely upon the moral principles of the farmer as a group. The farmer who puts poor apples or potatoes in the middle of the barrel, who uses false weights and measures, who fails to produce the best of which he is capable, lowers the price of all farm products. The dealer who must throw out a certain proportion of bad eggs in his miscellaneous purchases makes the buying price low enough to protect himself. The consumer's demand is gauged very largely by the quality or reliability of the goods he purchases. So dishonesty in farm business hurts the farmer more than it does anyone else. The minister can render a service when he imbues his people with the highest ideals of business morality.

Moreover, he can help in eliminating the loss to the farmer through attempted sale of [Pg 61] ungraded, miscellaneous products by encouraging standardization and guarantee of quality. This requires organization; and while it should be the pastor's aim to encourage the formation of agencies independent of the church to attend to this and to establish contacts between his community and State and independent organizations that will assist in this work he should not hesitate so far as his time will permit to organize such standardization work and organization for guaranteeing products until other agencies can take the work over. His obligation as community leader extends to the encouragement of every phase of life that makes the country more livable in the way demanded at the particular stage of development in which he finds the community.

As stated before, his primary task in encouraging production is now that of establishing contacts with State agencies and encouraging the support of their work. In some sections of the country, as among the colored people, for example, a country preacher might well be a trained farmer capable of doing in a local community what a county agent tries to do on a larger scale. [Pg 62] But the State has now progressed in most sections to the point where, if opportunity is offered, it can assist in this work and relieve the pastor for other duties.

The rural pastor should be a leader in community economic organization. It is accepted now that economic organizations along cooperative lines should be independent of either educational, religious, or social groups. After such organizations are well established the pastor has met in this respect the challenge to the church and to the pastor as community leader.

The church as a whole should have some form of organization whereby it can register its influence in favor of State legislation making safe the development of the cooperative movement, the better organization of marketing, the proper control of land ownership, taxation, and other business relations affecting the farmer. Many of these problems cannot be solved by a minister working alone in a local community. He can preach honesty, stability, loyalty to community organization with all the fervor and liberty of a prophet, but so long as the tenant contract remains an inducement to transient tenant [Pg 63] population; so long as class distinctions continue to become more marked; so long as discontent over high rents, high prices of land, and other conditions continues, he will not get far toward the establishing of the kingdom of heaven in agricultural life. These problems must be attacked by the church as a whole as the obligation of the general church to the minister who is on the firing line of the great world-wide struggle for the establishment of industrial peace.

One or two concrete illustrations will show the necessity of general church action on these matters if the rural church is to be saved from conditions now acute in the large centers. Wage-earners in the large centers who have no assurance of permanence of jobs are not inclined to give liberally toward providing adequate building and equipment for religious services. No wage-earner can be expected to give hundreds of dollars out of his income toward building a church when the next month may find him compelled to move to some distant city. In like manner it is difficult in large centers to get wage-earners even to maintain a church adequately. Consequently the church is to-day [Pg 64] spending millions of dollars to provide church buildings for wage-earners in large cities. Yet it does not have any program for bringing about wage returns, permanency of employment, or interest in business that would make it possible or desirable for the wage-earner to finance his own church building. Neither does the church have a plan whereby the industries of a city make any adequate contribution to the housing of religious institutions for those connected with the industry. Although the wealth of America is centered in the great cities, the provision for religious service to city people is being made by people living in small towns and in the open country.

As in the city, so in the open country. It has become necessary for the general church to provide even pastoral maintenance in certain sections where land is worth three hundred dollars per acre. The transient tenant has no abiding interest in the community because he expects to move at the end of the year. This condition is gradually becoming worse; and unless the general church undertakes the solution of problems affecting the local church but over which the local church [Pg 65] has no control, the future will bring either a decline in religious influence in rural sections or a continuous burden on national boards that should and would under proper conditions be cared for by local communities.

That the church can help in improving economic conditions to the advantage of all rural life has already been abundantly demonstrated. On the Brookhaven District, Mississippi Conference, Methodist Episcopal Church, the missionary board of that denomination made a contribution of three hundred dollars toward the support for the summer of a man and woman engaged in organizing community clubs. Twenty-one clubs were organized, and as a result of their efforts over fifty thousand pounds of fruit and truck were saved during the period of the war when food conservation was a necessity. As a result of this contribution, at last reports there were three colored county agricultural agents employed in counties of that district, all supported by the State, and no further contribution of missionary funds to continue the work was necessary. For years Bishop Thirkield, of the New Orleans area of the Methodist Episcopal Church, had [Pg 66] been encouraging keeping of gardens by the pastors and land ownership among colored people. It is impossible to estimate accurately the results of his broad program, but one district superintendent reported for his own official boards that while at the opening of the year 25 per cent of his official board members on the district were in debt, at the close of the year not one of them was in debt. They had been taught how to save money and to pay their debts, and the members of the churches were encouraged to follow their example.

On a little charge in southeastern Ohio the pastor began to preach good roads. Before the end of the first year a township organization had been formed and a vote taken providing for the macadamizing of every road in the township.

Four years ago the missionary board of the Methodist Episcopal Church made a contribution of four hundred dollars toward the support of a pastor in a village in New York. He organized a community club, led in securing a community house, installed moving pictures, and provided for the recreational life of the community. To-day no [Pg 67] contribution is being made by the Board for this work. Yet the membership of the club has increased from fifty-nine to two hundred and twenty-five. It has been responsible for the establishment of a national bank which had one hundred and seventy thousand dollars deposits in the first six months; it paved over five hundred feet of street; it provided for the consolidation of four rural schools with the village school. And plans were under way for opening a ferry across the Hudson that had not been run for thirty years and for the establishment of an important manufacturing plant. Thus a little stimulation has resulted in economic development that must result in better financial support of all community activities.

In conclusion it may be said that it is the business of the pastor to concern himself with all economic problems that affect the welfare of his people. The type of problem will vary with the community and its stage of development. As rapidly as possible the church should turn over to private or State agencies the task of economic development. But the church should encourage in every way every movement that is destined to bring about a [Pg 68] higher stage of economic welfare; and the pastor cannot relinquish his obligations in this respect until he has succeeded in establishing other agencies that can effectively perform this task. His duty, then, is to encourage this form of development by educating the people as to its value and by giving it his moral support.

[Pg 69]

CHAPTER IV

THE SOCIAL CHALLENGE TO THE CHURCH

The task of the minister is primarily to deal with man, either in his own personal life, his relations to his Maker, or to his fellow-man. Unlike the farmer, whose interest lies in the control of animal or plant growth, or the mechanic, who controls and molds the forces and conditions of inanimate nature, the minister has to do with that most delicate and elusive subject of all—the human soul. His business is to tune the individual soul instrument so that it will harmonize with the musical vibrations of the Infinite Will; and to bring about such a relationship between the different instruments in his little group that all together will produce a heavenly harmony.

The Christian religion, except when it has degenerated into formal Pharisaism, has been an ethical religion; and the ethical conduct of the individual has been a criterion of [Pg 70] the depth of his religious experience. Ethics have primarily to do with the relation of man to man, so that the conclusion is logical that the church is vitally interested in the ethical problems of humanity and in anything that tends to lower or raise the moral standards of the individual or the community.

There is no other agency more vitally interested in moral problems than is the church. Business organizations may be interested, but their efforts have apparently not been to conserve moral standards, even in business. The school is interested, but its emphasis has been placed more on mental development without regard to moral implications, or on utilitarian objectives. The church has been preaching right living, and other objectives have been incidental. Since this is true the thesis is advanced as the basis for this chapter that it is the business of the church to provide building, equipment, and leadership for conserving the moral life of the community. Since the moral welfare of any community finds its expression largely in its social and recreational activities, such provision involves providing for the social and recreational interests. This is a function [Pg 71] which is not to be encouraged and then turned over to other agencies, but is to be retained by the church itself as its legitimate service.

In view of the fact that the efforts of various agencies have not been in entire harmony with this point of view it deserves further consideration. For many years it has been argued that the schoolhouse should be so built that it could be made the community center for all types of activities. Without intending to limit the public schools in any laudable endeavor to enrich rural life it should be noted:

1. That so far as villages and open country schools are concerned it is not believed that the agitation for the wider use of the school plant has yet resulted in any marked nation-wide response to such agitation further than to provide room for physical training of upper-class students.

2. In general, the schoolhouse is so located that it is not suited for community service. It is usually located on the outskirts of the village, where plenty of ground may be had for outdoor school games. When people gather for social life and leisure they do not [Pg 72] go away from the lights of the village street but move toward them. The well-lighted poolroom near the village store will attract more boys than the building on the village edge that must be reached through the dark. Villagers have their downtown as well as do the great urban centers.

3. The school teachers and principal are busy five days in the week in the classroom. The schools cannot assume charge of community center activities without danger either of overworking the teachers or of having to hire special assistance for this service. Many villages cannot afford to hire special workers for this purpose alone.

4. It has been argued that the school is the democratic institution since it is tax-supported, and thus every one may go there as a right. To this it may be replied that, as with the church, only those contribute who have resources from which to contribute. The only difference is that in the public school the majority decide that all those who are able must contribute to the support of public institutions, thus it falls short of complete democracy, which must, in the last analysis, be a purely voluntary association. In [Pg 73] the church the only force compelling contribution is personal desire and public opinion. Thus it is as democratic, if not more so, than the school.

5. On the other hand, a large part of the time of the country minister is available for pastoral service. The establishment of community service activities under the auspices of the church bids fair to rescue pastoral calling and service from a routine of personal visitation by giving it a definite community service objective. Again, in the beginnings in the medium-sized and larger villages and probably continuously in the smaller places the pastor is the only salaried servant of the community with free time during the week for the organization and direction of community service.

6. The church building and parish house can be located conveniently at the center of the village, thus obviating the objection to the school building for this purpose.

7. True religion is a loyal supporter of everything that is safe in social and recreational life. It is subject to the control of the community in the same way as the school; excessive puritanism need not be feared [Pg 74] under its auspices more than under the auspices of other agencies.

The usual argument against serious consideration of the church as the center of community life is that religious agencies are so divided up by dogmatism that it is impossible for any one religious organization to assume leadership in this respect without incurring the opposition of other agencies. While this is true in many cases, it should be remembered that dogmatism does not have the influence in more highly developed communities that it once had. Moreover, considerable progress has already been made toward intergroup agreements, including the two great divisions of the Christian Church giving responsibility for community leadership to one denomination or another. In cases where local adjustments have not been made it may be necessary to depend on other agencies to conserve the social and recreational life. In these cases the church loses its rightful heritage.

8. The popular response to projects of building community churches and parish houses in small communities leads to the belief that the general public accepts as the [Pg 75] correct one the principle that the church should provide these facilities. The Methodist Episcopal denomination alone, through the aid of its Church Extension Board, aided in 1920 in building or remodeling over four hun-

dred church and parish houses equipped to provide for all or a part of a community service program; it is not known how many more made such advances without outside aid. The question of whether the church or some other agency than either the church or the school should provide community service facilities may be answered in much the same way. In some States local communities may levy a tax for the building and maintenance of community buildings. Where this is possible there seems to be no serious objection to such a course. But a community building without adequate supervision is likely to become a center of moral deterioration. On the other hand, such a public building can be located more strategically than can a schoolhouse. The objection to stock-company-owned community houses is much more serious. These are likely to become mere pleasure resorts, often of a very questionable nature.

[Pg 76]

The judgment of the American people seems to be rapidly determining that the safest plan is to look to the religious agencies for conserving the social and recreational life; and this judgment is in harmony with the thesis advanced at the opening of this chapter.

If the principle is accepted that it is the business of the church to conserve the social life of the community, then it is next in order to consider some of the problems of social life that are a challenge to the church at the present time.

The social organization of this country in its smaller communities as in the larger centers, such as it is, is the product of undirected uncoordinated efforts of special interest groups. A general classification of the types of rural organizations may be made, first, into political, including the incorporated village, towns, townships, counties, and political parties; economic, including special associations around specific interests such as farm bureaus, stock breeders' associations, potato-growers' associations, etc., and the increasing number of cooperative organizations, such as farmers' elevators, fruit-marketing [Pg 77] organizations, live-stock, shipping associations; social, including the Grange, the various types of farmers' clubs for men and women that perform much the same function as the Grange, and the more or less permanent groupings for purely recreational purposes, such as dancing parties, card parties, etc.;

and the conventional religious organizations as represented by the denominations and their many subsidiary groups for special purposes.

As was pointed out in the chapter on definitions, each of these various groups has a customary center for coming together. But owing to the fact that each interest has grown largely without reference to the others, their centers of activity have been determined largely by conditions of local convenience. Now, these centers may have been well adapted to the times when they were established, but as time has passed shifts of population have come, road improvements have been made, and new interests developed so that the traditional centers not only tend to lessen community solidarity but also tend to prevent its accomplishment. One of the first tasks of the community leader is to [Pg 78] make a study of his proposed field of activity for the purpose of determining what are the present centers of group interests, what changes have taken place in rural life conditions which make reorganization and readjustment of centers desirable, and then, in consultation with representatives of the community, to organize a community plan toward ward which the entire community may work. City planning has long been an accepted principle for service in the more progressive larger centers. The time has come when plans for the most efficient organization of village and open country communities should be made. It is interesting to note that already in many sections of the United States the movement toward community planning has made considerable progress. It is now generally recognized that with rare exceptions the village rather than an open country point is the normal basis for such a plan. In accordance with this, movements are now under way to displace the traditional township boundaries created as political limits for government and to replace them by boundaries conforming as closely as possible with those limits that careful [Pg 79] investigation indicates are now and probably will continue to be the most representative of what the future limits of rural communities will be. In like manner educational work is being reorganized to include the community territory instead of the political areas inherited from the methods of survey adopted under the ordinance of 1787. As this movement continues, doubtless farm bureaus, and even religious agencies, will try to adapt themselves as far as possible to the program of other agencies.

The breakdown of social life in the open country and the very questionable forms it often takes in the villages has long been the nightmare of the minister of the gospel who stands for a high ethical plane of social life. The church, with its Ladies' Aid, its young people's societies, its occasional men's clubs, fails to reach more than a very limited number of those living in the open country or in the village. The lack of a definite, well-organized social program results in all kinds of association often anti-social and lowering of the moral fiber of the entire group. It is unnecessary to go into the sordid details of moral conditions existing among both young [Pg 80] and old in many village communities. The pastor with a program of absentee service consisting of an occasional sermon and holding a Sunday school finds his efforts continually nullified by more powerful social and recreational impulses expressing themselves in ways recognized as morally deteriorating. When a plan for ultimate centralization of wholesome and legitimate community interest has been made it is the minister's task to organize a plan for bringing to the community an abundance of wholesome recreational life. The traditional plan has been to preach against dancing and card playing. Such preaching has more often alienated the young people from the church than it has attracted them to religious life. The modern plan is to overcome evil with good; that is, to provide such a program of unquestioned recreation that the evil will die of itself.

That this actually happens has been demonstrated over and over again. The Rev. Matthew B. McNutt, on arriving at Du Page, Illinois, found a large building near the church turned into a dancing center. Without saying a word against dancing he [Pg 81] began to organize his young people for singing. In a short time the dancing mania had ceased and did not return in the twelve years of his service on that charge. The Rev. L. P. Fagan found dancing all the rage when he went to a little town in Colorado. He began to develop a wholesome program of recreational life, and before long dancing had ceased and had not returned two years after he had left the charge. At a little town in New York State, the young men of the town were accustomed to gather at the fire house and indulge in cards with more than occasional playing for money. A recreation hall opened in the village broke up the card-playing and brought the young men into something more wholesome and which they preferred. A village in Southwestern Ohio had a gang of "Roughnecks," as they were called, who were accustomed to loaf in the poolrooms and find their amusement in neighboring cities. A room in the upstairs of the town hall was opened up and fitted for basketball. Leadership for clubs was provided by college students training for community service. The result was that this group of young men, of exceptionally good [Pg 82] native qualities but spoiling morally for want of adequate provision for recreational life, came to the community center and for the time being avoided the lower forms of social and recreational activity.

These illustrations prove three things: first, the need of such equipment; second, the fact that young people prefer and choose the better when it is provided for them; and, third, that the church can solve many of its most serious problems most readily by attacking the source of corruption of the morals of young people through caring for recreational interests. The minister who neglects this powerful force in attempting to build a Christian civilization is failing to take advantage of one of the greatest instruments God has placed in his hands. Yet it is the sad fact that in too many instances ministers are failing to take advantage of the forces at hand, and that even those who have caught the vision of the possibilities of these other forces are not trained to use them safely.

The number of village communities that have organized social and recreational life is still so small that when such movements are discovered they receive widespread [Pg 83] comment in the public press. One can drop into almost any village in America and make inquiries as to what is being done for conserving the recreational life by the church or any other community agency, and the answer will be that nothing is done either in providing leadership or buildings and equipment. Much good work has been done for specific groups by the Christian Associations, and now the American Playground Association, the Red Cross, and other organizations are applying themselves to the task of bringing about a better condition in smaller communities. But the work accomplished by all of them is still, as compared with the task in hand, scarcely more than a beginning. The church with a paid community leader in each community offers the solution for most rapid and permanent progress; and the outlook for rapid development under religious auspices is most hopeful.

[Pg 84]

CHAPTER V

BUILDING FOR COMMUNITY SERVICE

The thesis that the church should provide building and equipment for conservation of the social and recreational life of the church introduces standards and objectives that do not find expression in the great majority of church buildings now erected, nor even in the majority of plans sent out by religious agencies or architectural concerns bidding for contracts for church planning and building.

The traditional village and open country church was a one-room structure erected for the sole purpose of providing a place for worship. This amply met the needs of a pioneer time when social activities were largely carried on in the homes. In a very large number of communities this is still the only type of church building to be found. As the idea of providing for Sunday school began to prevail gradually side rooms were added [Pg 85] to provide for extra Sunday school classes. In the course of time the needs of a wider program for the church began to be recognized, and then basements were added with an occasional kitchen. Thus the entertainments for adults and of the young people old enough to enjoy banquets and like amusement were provided for. But the needs of the young people under sixteen years of age and many other community needs were still uncared for.

The new program demands a building or buildings that will provide for the threefold program of worship, religious education, and community service. In view of the lack of standards for rural church building, the present discussion is offered in the hope that it may contain some practical suggestions in terms of the program demanded of the modern open country and village church.

It is believed that the type of building suitable for an open country community will be somewhat different from that needed in a village center. The number of rooms will be less. Usually, two main rooms, one for worship and the other for recreational purposes, with such side rooms for kitchen and [Pg 86] special clubs and classes as the community can afford, will be sufficient. The recreation room should have stage, lantern slide, and moving picture equipment, and a very simple provision for games. Problems of plumbing and heating must be worked out in accordance with local conditions.

In the larger centers, in addition to the facilities mentioned above, other rooms may be added as a careful study of village equipment and needs, present and probable future, indicate. Rooms for library, committees, clubs, offices, shower baths, lockers, art center, and similar interests should be provided for if other agencies have not done so.

In building for community service the community should not make the mistake of economizing because it imagines it cannot afford the best. No community should build less than the best. If it does so, it handicaps the community for a generation or more; and this is too serious a matter to be lightly permitted. At the present time religious organizations have national agencies which are serving to an ever larger degree as a reserve resource for the purpose of aiding local groups to build adequately. Thus the general [Pg 87] organization aids each year the limited number of local groups that find it necessary to rebuild and renders unnecessary the maintenance of a replacement fund by the local church for an indefinite period.

If it is impossible to build an entire building at one time it is better to build by units, so that in the course of time a structure of which the community may be proud will be completed. It should be remembered that a community's solidarity and spirit are gauged largely by the type of buildings it erects, and the church and community building, representing as it does the deepest interests of man, should be a living monument to community loyalty. Such a building becomes a lasting inspiration to both old and young, pointing the way to the highest and best in human life.

The building should be strategically located. As has been suggested, people like to come to the center of the village for their social and recreational life. The owner of a poolroom or a picture show that would place his building a half mile in the country would not have a large and enthusiastic patronage. The main street, near the center of [Pg 88] the village, is the place to be selected for the principal building of the city, the community center.

Sometimes a well-meaning citizen will offer to a church a plot of land far out on the edge of a village free of charge, provided the church will accept it for the erection of the new structure. Sometimes the Board of Trustees, thinking they will save a few hundred dollars, gratefully accept the gift, thus violating the principle expressed in the preceding paragraph. When a business man plans to put up an expensive building he does not seek the cheapest land but the best location regardless of the cost of the land. For illustration, a lot on the edge of a village may cost but five hundred dollars, while a lot in the center of the village may cost five thousand dollars. If the proposed building to be erected is to cost fifty thousand dollars, even the larger land cost is but ten per cent of the total; and the value of the building to the community after erection on the more valuable lot far more than justifies the extra expenditure.

Sometimes architects are inclined to sacrifice utility to beauty. They are inclined to [Pg 89] make the recreation room too short because a proper length would not harmonize with other lines in the building. The good architect accepts the beautification of a useful building as a challenge and does not sacrifice utility because a useful structure does not embody some feature of Gothic or Old English parish church architecture. This tendency should be carefully guarded against.

Details as to the slope of ground best adapted to church building, heating, plumbing, and other features can best be learned by consultation with a trained architect. Care should be taken to see that the recreation room is sufficiently large to carry on the simpler games, such as basketball, when the community so desires. The limits recommended are fourteen feet high by forty feet wide by sixty feet long. Many communities, however, are getting along with rooms considerably shorter and narrower than this. The ceiling should be supported by steel beams instead of posts. In most sections of the country it is recommended that recreation rooms be erected on the same level as the church instead of in the basement, as has been the practice.

[Pg 90]

In many sections of the country there is a distinct objection to having the community service features and the house of worship under the same roof. It is thought that the light-heartedness of play time tends to lessen the sacredness of the house of worship and to lessen respect for religious service. While this attitude is largely a matter of custom, and while people who have caught the vision of God can worship him any place, it is believed that wherever possible consideration should be given to this sentiment and the community service features of the church should be housed in a separate building located adjacent to the church or attached to it by some smaller club room. The two should not be located in widely separate parts of the village, as the connection between the two may be lost and the service of the church to the community in this way not recognized. Both house of worship and community or parish house should be located near the center of the village.

In villages where there is room for several houses of worship the question of community service is much more difficult. The Young Men's Christian Associations and the [Pg 91] Young Women's Christian Associations have made partial provision in some communities on an interdenominational basis. But in the ordinary small town there is not room for a building for each of these organizations. The rural Christian Associations have been proceeding on the policy of using such buildings as are now available, but it is evident that in the vast majority of small communities, present buildings can at best be but a makeshift for complete community service. It is hoped that the time will come when the several denominations will find some way of pooling their financial resources so that as religious organizations they can provide a common building for community service. The writer knows of no village in America where this has yet been done. One village in New York State, Milton-on-the-Hudson, has a community club under the direction of a Board of Trustees of ten members, two from each of the five denominations represented in the village, the Catholic church included. This club has been very successful in operating a community house and developing a community program. It has been suggested that where property [Pg 92] rights are involved one denomination might make its contribution by providing and maintaining the building, while the other denominations might contribute the equivalent of interest on building investment, depreciation and maintenance of building to cost of operation of the plant. It is feared, however, that in the course of time, the original cost of building to one denomination would be forgotten and the community would demand that all groups contribute to operating expenses according to their membership or some other agreed upon distribution of maintenance expense. This should be the ultimate method of maintenance.

In a number of communities one denomination has provided the building and the operating force, while other denominations have cooperated by acting on the Board of Control and contributing what they could to the maintenance cost. Such denominational leadership almost invariably leads in the beginning to interdenominational jealousy and antagonism, but in some cases the community has accepted the situation and all have cooperated, it being understood that such provision for community purposes is [Pg 93] not for the purpose of proselyting. Sunday school and church membership is encouraged in the denominations from which the young people come, and thus a contribution by one denomination has strengthened the work of all the churches. Some form of cooperation agreed upon for a common development is preferable and independent action by one denomination should be undertaken only when the different groups concerned are not in a position either by tradition or financial ability to cooperate in a common enterprise.

The movement now is very strong in the direction of provision of building and equipment for community service by the church. May the church not fail in doing justice to its high obligation in the type of structure it may erect!

[Pg 94]

CHAPTER VI

THE CHURCH AND RURAL PUBLIC THOUGHT

Many city pastors, and some rural ones too, lament the fact that people do not come to listen to them preach. This condition is in marked contrast to the good old New England days, when the whole neighborhood would turn out and listen to sermons four hours long. It is a question whether such intellectual giants as Jonathan Edwards built up such congregations or whether such congregations brought out the best in Jonathan Edwards.

People to-day go to church for a variety of reasons. But the dominant motives that should prevail are those of worship and for instruction. All Christians should attend religious services for worship regardless of the quality of the sermon or the personal attitude of the people toward the minister. The message from the pulpit should be such that it too would attract for its own sake. [Pg 95] It is the exceptional city minister that can fill the pews from week to week and from year to year because of the type of message given. The daily papers and the many other agencies for discussion of live topics have become so numerous that the pulpit has lost much of its original importance as an agency for instruction. But in the village and the open country the pulpit still has a large field for service in this respect and thus becomes an especial challenge to the one who wants to develop as a leader of thought. The village minister has an opportunity unique in American life in this respect. Some of the greatest leaders of thought ever produced were the product of the village churches of England and Scotland. There is no reason why the village church of America should not become the seedbed for the best contributions to religious, philosophical, and literary thought of the present day.

It will be impossible to give more than a few illustrations of present needs and opportunities for service in this respect in the smaller communities. One of the first tasks of the church is the introduction of correct thought in regard to religious beliefs. It is [Pg 96] almost unbelievable the amount of actual superstition and positively harmful beliefs that prevail under the guise of religion not only in rural but in urban communities. An example of this is the widespread belief in the second coming of Christ at an early date. Educational institutions of national note are continuously laboring to extend this form of belief. The question as to whether Christ will ever come again is one that does not appear to have any immediate social significance other than it may have some influence on conduct as to the method of preparation for his coming. Those who believe in such coming may either believe that all efforts at social improvement now are fruitless, because the ultimate inauguration of the Kingdom will result from the sweeping away of everything that now exists and in the inauguration of a new social order out of the ruins of the old. Or they may believe that the efforts of the churches and other agencies now are preparing the way for such coming, and the inauguration of the Kingdom will be but the next step in an orderly process of social progress. There is reason to believe that many of those who are teaching [Pg 97] the second coming are inclined to the former point of view; and wherever they gain a hearing their influence practically nullifies all efforts to enlist their followers in any program of social improvement.

The effect of a belief in an immediate coming of Christ as indicated by present world conditions interpreted in the light of Old and New Testament prophecy is to paralyze all motive for social action. Such action, if this belief is correct, is useless. The devotee is driven to the position of finding his sole religious duty that of getting himself and those in whom he is interested ready to enter the new kingdom through the observance of the personal elements in religious life.

Another belief that in some sections has a limited influence is that of observance of Saturday instead of Sunday as the day set apart by biblical authority as the Sabbath. Without commenting on the rightness or the wrong of the contention, it should be remembered that this belief has resulted in some sections in practically the breakdown of observance of the Sabbath by rural communities, without a corresponding gain in Saturday observance. Community solidarity [Pg 98] for either social or religious purposes is thus broken up. From the social point of view this is distinctly unfortunate.

Again, in some sections religion has taken an extreme form of antagonism to anything of a practical type. The extremes to which the emotional expression of religion has gone have been such that these groups have become popularly known as "Holy Rollers." Wherever this type of religious expression breaks out in a rural community it severely handicaps all efforts at making the church function as an agency for rural progress. The energies of such devotees are so exhausted in their services that they lack the energy, even if they had the inspiration, to link their efforts to any program of community betterment. This group is usually found not only opposing progressive measures in the church but also opposing other progressive activities in the community, such as better schools, road improvement, etc.

In isolated sections of rural America all over the country may be found groups of Latter Day Saints. These groups are not yet of sufficient strength to be of great importance outside of Utah and a few other [Pg 99] Western States. But the existence of an organized group anywhere, particularly if it is of a missionary character, is likely to spread and ultimately become a factor of considerable importance. Anyone visiting the Mormon Temple at Salt Lake and reading on the monuments to Joseph and Hiram Smith the testimony in letters of stone to the effect that Joseph discovered the message of the Book of Mormon on gold plates, and that Hiram was the witness thereof, will realize how easy it is to spread almost any belief under the guise of religion if the children are taught such doctrines during their youth.

It will be unnecessary to go through the whole catalogue of beliefs finding expression in the dogma of practically all religious organizations, and in times past dividing the followers of Christianity into denominational groups. The most serious problems of adjustment of religious institutions for community service grow out of these differences in belief on points of dogma.

The solution of the problem of clearing the field of unwholesome and injurious belief lies not in writing polemics against them but in filling the minds of the people with [Pg 100] unquestioned truth. As the rural mind is directed to the consideration of topics of vital importance these things that have crept in and disturbed social order and dissipated precious energies in fruitless discussion will disappear through lack of attention. On the other hand, persecution will attract attention to and arouse the fanatical support of them and distract the attention of the group from matters of more vital importance.

In addition to preaching those sermons which keep alive in community consciousness the sense of man's obligations to his Maker, the significance and solemnity of death and those other epochal events in the course of human existence, and the hope given to man of a fuller life through the coming of Christ, the minister has certain great moral ideals that he should instill into the minds of his people.

The matter of honesty in dealing with both the farmer and his neighbors both near and distant has already been mentioned.

The right attitude toward wealth accumulation must also be preached not only for the safety of the rural community but also for [Pg 101] the entire nation. By the very nature of the business the vast majority of people living in small communities and on the farms must remain indefinitely people of modest means. The possibilities of large wealth accumulation are limited because the farm must continue to be a small scale industry. It can be improved so as to afford adequate leisure. But farm life does not promise large enjoyment to those of an epicurean turn of mind. The ideal of the farm must be that of producing wealth so that the modest comforts of life may be insured. But the minister must exalt the appreciation of those things that may be obtained without lavish expenditure of money, such as local entertainment produced by the community itself, literature, music, and art; and the simple pleasures that come from democratic association with intimate acquaintances.

It is believed that with all the material progress of this country, it has had to sacrifice many things that are worth far more than the types of enjoyment obtained by slavish imitation of the extremely wealthy leisure class in the cities. The exhortation to preach the values of the simple pleasures [Pg 102] possible in smaller communities is not for the purpose of keeping people contented with a lot that cannot be improved, but because it is believed that the smaller communities to-day contain within themselves and their ideals the seed of rejuvenation of all life, and that a greater contribution can be made by rural communities to civilization by adhering to their ideals than by being diverted from them by the money-seeking, mate-

60

rialistic ideals of the urban centers. The best in rural ideals must ultimately become the ideals of the city if we are to avoid the degeneration that will inevitably follow a too materialistic urban civilization.

The pastor should be able to bring to his people from time to time the interpretation of national and world events in terms of their relation to the advance of religious progress. This obligation will require constant and wide reading about the social movements of the time. In the more progressive communities many of the farmers and their families will have access to literature that will enable them to form their own conclusions to a large degree. But not many of them, even though they be college graduates, [Pg 103] will have the time to read as widely as they would like on any of the great changes taking place; and they will welcome an intelligent interpretation of these by the one who has the larger opportunities for such service.

Finally, the preacher must be a prophet. He must have caught the vision of tendencies in human life and be able to bring to his people the evidences of the hand of God working out the course of the human race in the infinite stream of human history. He must believe, with Tennyson, in a "far off divine event, toward which the whole creation moves," or with Shakespeare when he said "There's a divinity that shapes our ends, rough-hew them how we will." If he can bring his people to see that, even though they may be living in some obscure corner of the earth, they have a part in the great movements going on, and that they can render a service by doing what they are able in supporting the programs for which the church stands, he will be contributing his share to the wholesome attitude needed in our rural communities.

[Pg 104]

CHAPTER VII

ADJUSTING THE LOCAL CHURCH TO THE COMMUNITY

In his book on Social Control Professor Ross has pointed out that certain institutions are essentially conservative in their nature. They are solid, permanent organizations but are not inclined to assume leadership in social progress. He includes in this list the church. The fact that the church is a conservative institution is not necessarily a criticism of it. Other agencies develop new phases of social expression, sometimes in actual opposition to conservative agencies. The good innovations live and after they have demonstrated their utility the conservative institutions such as the church and the state take them over and insure their permanence.

The rapid advance of the social spirit in modern life has outstripped existing agencies in their preparation to meet the new [Pg 105] approach to the solution of problems of living. Many forms of existing institutions were created under entirely different conditions and to meet different needs. To-day these old forms do not adapt themselves to new demands, and in many cases prevent effective action on the part of religious organizations that are ready in spirit to broaden their programs to include the new demands upon the conservative organization.

The minister, trained for the modern service of the church to the community, cannot solve alone all the problems of maladjustment he finds in his local community. He finds that the contacts and interests of his local church organization are far broader than the interests of the local group he is called to serve; and that in many cases his local efforts are nullified by these larger contacts. It is the purpose of this and succeeding chapters to outline some of the conditions existing within the church itself that must be adjusted before it can act most effectively in meeting the challenge discussed in preceding chapters.

The first and probably most important problem is that of enlarging the vision of [Pg 106] church officials, ministers, and people as to the need for broadening the program of the church and as to the need of a statesman-like reorganization of adjustment of the church to the community.

It is believed that quite generally the membership of the larger religious organizations in this country are now in sympathy with the principle that the church should have a social-service program. There is still wide diversity of opinion as to the form that service should take. In too many cases there is no opinion at all; and while admitting the principle, active opposition develops to any attempt to put the principle into practice in a specific project. This condition is to be found most marked in those sections of the country that are not in the direct line of thought movements, or where living conditions are such as to make rural life monotonous. The monotony of the plains is as deadening as is the lack of contact of the mountain valley; and both fields offer fruitful ground for the spread of unsocial types of religious expression.

The solution of this phase of adjustment of the church to community needs lies in a [Pg 107] patient educational program carried on by the minister of the gospel. He must be a man of broad vision and must have the fullest appreciation of the slowness with which the rural public mind works. He must be everlastingly tactful and not attempt more than the simplest advances at the beginning and not more than one at a time. He should have at hand an abundance of educational material in the way of literature, lantern slides, and periodicals which can be used in showing what actually happens when the church embarks on a broader program of rural service. A national educational program of this type will in a few years create a demand that must be met and that rural churches will pay well for as the value of such work will be recognized.

The more serious phase of this problem is the lack of adequate preparation for this service on the part of the ministry. In one of the leading denominations (Methodist Episcopal) over twenty-nine per cent of the charges are cared for by supplies, men who by reason of educational preparation, age, or for some other cause are not now and, in a large proportion of cases, never will be [Pg 108] eligible to membership in the Conferences. Of the remainder, only a small proportion are graduates of schools of higher learning, such as colleges and theological seminaries. At a time when a large number of those living in rural communities are either agricultural college graduates or have attended short courses in agriculture, it becomes apparent that an uneducated ministry is becoming a menace to the future of the rural church.

But of those who have had the advantages of a college or theological seminary training, the type of training has not fitted them for effective rural service. The training of ministers has gone through the same process as other types of training. It was once thought that since the sole business of the minister was the personal appeal to accept Christ, with the emphasis on the personal atonement features of Christianity rather than on the principles of Christian living, the same type of training would fit one to deliver the message whether he was in the slums of the city, on the shores of Africa, or in the mountains of Colorado. Moreover, for some reason, it appears to have been [Pg 109] accepted that the rural ministry was the simplest of all and that any one could be a rural minister. It would be amusing if it were not so tragic to accept the testimony of some of those who have not yet seen that the rural ministry is a type demanding such a cosmopolitan understanding of human nature and of conditions of human existence that it demands the best intellects and the highest type of missionary spirit to carry on successfully. We have heard of college presidents recommending young men for important rural positions because the young man was "not ambitious for any important work in the church." It has been known that officials in the church would bid for theological seminary graduates with the assurance that while they would have to accept an "undesirable" rural charge for a year or so, they would soon be "promoted." The writer knows of at least one young Negro minister, a holder of a Master's degree from a large educational institution, whose major work for his higher degree was in the dead languages. The attitude of our educational institutions, and the attitude in public thought has been that progress for the individual has [Pg 110] been in the direction of getting away from the country instead of remaining with rural folk and giving one's life to the advancement of the group as a whole; and the courses of study have had primarily in mind the personal appeal rather than that of dealing with man in his particular environment.

It is now recognized that modern life demands a specialized ministry. The one who can handle successfully a rural industrial or a downtown urban situation may not be at all fitted to deal with the problems of the village or the open country. On the other hand, the one who can serve farmers successfully might not be at all fitted to fill a metropolitan pulpit. Beginnings only have been made in attempting to adjust educational work to meet this modern demand. In the meantime the problem remains of the ministers trained under former conditions, if trained at all. Many of them have not yet caught the vision of the larger program of the church; and of those who have caught this vision the handling of the tools of the new program is such a delicate task that many failures are sure to be recorded. It will take years to bring the church to the place where [Pg 111] it can meet successfully the modern demands upon it.

The second great problem is that of maladjustment in thought. Protestantism is still suffering from the effects of extreme individualism in religious belief. Strong leaders, obsessed with some one variation in interpretation of the Scriptures, have pulled off from the main body of the church and have started independent organizations committed to the development of the particular interpretation they have made. When once these organizations have been formed and have secured a financial backing, they have continued to spread, until to-day rural America presents the spectacle of religious forces agreeing on the broad general program of the relation of the church to community needs but paralyzed because of dissensions over less essential principles of theological dogma. The reasons for separate organizations have often been forgotten and loyalty to a particular organization as such has taken its place.

The solution of this problem is not that of attempting to eliminate differences in dogmatic belief by argument, but of emphasizing [Pg 112] the points of agreement of the various religious groups. Error and nonessential dividing lines will disappear if neglected. But if they are agitated, they will thrive under persecution and conditions will be worse than ever.

The third problem is that of maladjustment of buildings to community needs. This problem presents itself in two aspects: first, that of location of church buildings, and, second, that of location of pastors' residences. In the original settlement of this country, people located their new homes in neighborhoods partly for social and economic purposes and partly for protection. Where these new groups were founded the church building soon found a place. As the communities grew, and aided in the course of time by ambitious national agencies, the sectarian interests mentioned above established new churches to care for those of each particular belief until many communities soon became overchurched. The rapid decrease in open-country, and even village, population which began during the 70's of the past century and which has continued to the present made the problem still worse, [Pg 113] until to-day probably the least efficient institution in all rural life is the rural church.

Moreover, the first settlements did not always mark the spot of permanent development of population and interest centers. As time has passed, many of the places which it was once thought would be permanent centers have lost their preeminence and others have taken their place, until now many very small communities have too many churches, and others are lacking in adequate facilities for religious service.

The time has now come when it is believed that rural population and agricultural tendencies are sufficiently well known to enable those interested in rural life development to determine what are the most suitable centers for community development. The Interchurch World Movement, had it been carried to a successful conclusion, would have gone far toward determining those centers for the entire United States. As it is, the Movement made possible such determination for about one fifth of the United States and the task of completing the survey may be accomplished in the course of time.

When this task is completed, then the [Pg 114] challenge to the churches of America will be to so readjust the location of their church buildings and to remodel them in such a way as to be adapted to the present and probable future growth of communities so determined. This work is scarcely begun, but it is believed that it has gone far enough to insure its ultimate achievement. When this is done, then the local church will be in a position to deal most effectively with the community problems mentioned in preceding chapters.

The situation as to location of pastors' residences is even more serious than that of location of church buildings. During the pioneer period of church organization ministers were under the necessity of dividing their efforts among a considerable number of small groups. These were organized into circuits and the pastor's residence was provided at the point either where the original church was established or where it was most convenient for him to serve the preaching points under his care. Each denomination developed its own work regardless of other groups and in many cases from the same common center, so that we now have in rural and village organization pastors' residences [Pg 115] centralized in the minority of rural communities and the great majority of such communities without resident pastoral care.

In the State of Ohio, for example, in one county of twenty-four communities but twelve have resident pastors and in these twelve communities thirty-nine pastors reside. In another of sixteen communities but eight have resident pastors. Yet in each county there are enough ministers to supply each community with a resident pastor, if readjustment were to be made. In the northeastern part of the State on a single Methodist district are to be found two instances of Methodist and Presbyterian pastors living in the same village and going on alternate Sundays to another village, in one instance larger than that wherein the ministers live. The facts as to the growth and decline of churches with resident or non-resident ministers elsewhere present (see Church Growth and Decline in Ohio) are a sufficient indication of the effects of maladjustment of pastoral residences to rural community needs. Since the modern demand of rural life upon the church is for community leadership as well as for holding Sunday [Pg 116] worship, it is clear that no adequate program of church leadership in rural life can be worked out until this vital need of readjustment of pastoral residences to community service is met.

A third serious problem is that of lack of coordination of denominational effort in community service. Where two or more religious organizations find a place in the same small community, no plan has yet been successfully tried whereby these organizations as such have been brought into harmonious and continuous action for community service. The presence of two or three ministers of social vision in the same small community is not always an asset, since small communities do not have a place for more than one leader and sectarian interests forbid cooperation under the leadership of either of the church pastors. This situation has given rise to such organizations as the Christian Associations, the Sunday School Associations, and a large number of nonreligious agencies now trying to provide for community leadership independent of the church. It is intended here to call attention to the problem. A suggestion as to methods of solution [Pg 117] will be taken up more at length in a succeeding chapter.

A fourth serious problem resulting from the above is lack of adequate support for rural religious institutions. Owing to the general lack of financial resources of rural communities as compared with the urban centers, they have not been able to compete financially with city churches in bidding for men who have high standards of living and who demand large financial returns for services rendered. This condition will probably continue indefinitely because of the tendency of large-scale industrial production to centralize wealth control in urban centers; that is, unless the economic motive is taken from Christian service through the equalization of salaries. This is a solution much to be desired, but it is feared that pastors will not take kindly to such a movement; and members of city churches will continue to contribute to the support of their own particular pastor instead of to general pastoral support. But the weakness in support has been seriously increased because of dividing of such resources as rural communities have among so many different agencies. Many [Pg 118] communities that could support a pastor at two thousand dollars or more a year now have men serving denominations at one thousand dollars per year or less.

The same is true of church building. When five church buildings must be erected and maintained for sectarian purposes in a town where there is room for but one school building there is little wonder that the contrast between church buildings and other rural institutional buildings is so marked. And it is little wonder that when people begin to think in community terms they are inclined to pass by the church as an institution offering hope of community service conservation and turn either to the school or to some other agency that they hope will serve the purpose.

Closely akin to the problem of inadequate support for the country minister and the country church is that contention often made that the job of a country preacher does not offer as great a challenge as does that of service in other branches of church work. It is believed that this contention is erroneous because the rural work, while not demanding the same qualities of service as other types, [Pg 119] does demand qualities of its own that equal, if they do not exceed, those of the city pulpit. The ability to serve people long and continuously in close personal relation to them; to deal patiently with conservatism; to endure the hardships of living under conditions far below what are to be found in city environments; to get the support of the people for progressive measures, and to keep alive mentally in an environment that is not the most conducive to study because of lack of reading facilities and because of the ease with which one may shirk the means of personal growth—all these make the task one for the specially capable and devoted.

But if there is truth in the statement that the country ministry does not offer the opportunity for the exercise of personal abilities required by the city pulpit, then, unless we frankly recognize that the limit of possibility of building up the rural work is to alleviate an unavoidable discrepancy in personal challenge, it becomes necessary to so reorganize the local parish that it will be a challenge fit to attract the best minds in the church.

The first step already has been mentioned: [Pg 120] that is, to adjust relationships between denominations so that a minister will have sole responsibility for community leadership.

The second is to enlarge the parishes under the control of one pastor that he will have ample field for the exercise of his abilities. In some sections of the country two or more communities may still have to be assigned to one minister, with the expectation that he will develop local volunteer leadership in the respective communities, or have adequate assistance in the way of special workers among the children and in the homes and have directors of religious education for full or part time in each community. In most sections of the country the communities are now of such a size as to demand the full time of a paid minister and to pay a satisfactory salary for services rendered.

The third is to increase the functions of the pastorate so that people will be willing to pay more for the service rendered. This results directly from the adoption of the larger program for the church herein recommended.

The practice—still all too rare—of [Pg 121] supplying the pastor with an automobile for pastoral work, should be encouraged everywhere, particularly when the charge has a pastor who has the vision of the broader program of the church and is specially trained for his work. There are complications in the connectional system of making appointments that tend to prevent liberality in this respect. When a charge is brought up to adequate self-support the tendency is too often to make the charge a place to "take care" of a Conference member of that grade regardless of his fitness to follow up the type of program introduced by his predecessor. The taking of the automobile by the departing pastor deprives the community of its use. Leaving it for the use of an inefficient pastor is too great a burden on the community. Experience will determine the best means of handling this problem and should ultimately put ministers on the same basis as to having means of transportation furnished as County Agricultural Agents, County Superintendents of Schools, Christian Association Secretaries, etc.

The soldier in the ranks will probably never be looked upon as in the same grade [Pg 122] of responsible position as the captain of the company. So the country minister has a right to look forward in due time to "promotion" in natural channels; that is, to the district superintendency. It is to be feared that too often at the present time, the rural minister is discouraged from remaining in the rural work because he sees that a very large proportion of the positions in the church that are recognized as personal promotions are filled from the city pulpits. His course of advance is now from the country pulpit to the city pulpit, thence to the district superintendency or detached service, thence to the bishopric, a position very few ministers refuse if offered. The rural work would be strengthened if rural district superintendencies were filled by rural men who have demonstrated their ability to build up a rural charge successfully, and then if these same rural district superintendents were to have an opportunity to fill the highest possible positions in the church, thus bringing to the highest administrative offices of the church the tried experience that comes from building up a district in Methodism. When the necessity of leaving the rural work [Pg 123] in order to get "promotion" is eliminated there will be a marked strengthening of loyalty to the rural work.

The illustrations given have been taken from Methodist Episcopal experience. Other denominations have similar problems, but probably to a less degree because of the more marked form of localized democracy in church polity.

If the churches of America permit this crisis of lack of adjustment of church to community needs to pass unchallenged, and if they delay in making the adjustments needed, the time will soon come when other agencies, supported by rural communities, will make provision for these needs and the opportunity of the church will be gone indefinitely. Other agencies will be performing a real Christian service, and the church, by reason of its failure to live up to the demands upon it, will have an increasingly difficult task of justifying its existence so far as relationship to this world is concerned.

[Pg 124]

CHAPTER VIII

INTERDENOMINATIONAL READJUSTMENT

Rural progress under church leadership has been much like the first drops of water on a placid lake at the beginning of a rain. Little rises of water appear and some waves circle out, but the ultimate level is not much raised. So with the church. Here and there a minister stirs up some local community, some definite progress is made, attention is attracted from other communities and they may have a few symptoms of a rise, but too often the minister moves, another comes, and the general level of community life falls back to what it was before.

The difficulty is that with the overlapping of interdenominational jurisdictions it is impossible for any group to lead in progress outside of the local community. Methodists cannot lead in a county program because Baptists and Presbyterians will not follow them. Neither can the other groups lead [Pg 125] because Methodists are not gifted in following the leadership of other denominations. It is perfectly natural and justifiable that this should be so. Before the churches of America, Protestant or Catholic, can render the entire service demanded of them there must be a thoroughgoing system of interdenominational cooperation worked out which will insure joint responsibility of all denominations concerned in providing for community leadership on a large scale. If this is impossible, then the inevitable alternative must be accepted of passing by the churches of America in carrying out comprehensive plans of progress and of turning to other agencies for this service.

During the past, largely owing to the apparently hopeless situation so far as interdenominational cooperation is concerned, Christian organizations, such as Christian Associations and Sunday School Associations, have sprung up to do for the denominations and for the ministers what they could not do under present conditions. These agencies have done notable work. They have accomplished much in preparing the way for a nation-wide recognition of what [Pg 126] the broad function of the church is; they have brought representatives of all denominations together and have gradually increased the social spirit while at the same time lessening the emphasis upon those things which have divided the Christian Church into so many isolated camps. They have pioneered and experimented. They have had failures as well as successes, but their failures have been a real contribution to the sum total of human experience and have taught us many things that should be avoided. The service rendered by these agencies must ever be remembered as of the most vital and important character.

But it will be admitted by representatives of all organizations that a large part of what is now found in the programs of those other religious organizations, "arms" of the church, is a legitimate part of the work that should be supervised by the minister of a community program and included in his program, and that in those communities where such trained pastoral leadership exists the functions of these other agencies can be materially modified and their activities directed into still further new and untried [Pg 127] fields of endeavor. The church needs organizations supported from funds not coming through the regular channels founded on the budgets of individual churches. These subsidiary organizations can go ahead with experimentation, and their failures do not bring the discredit to the parent organization that they would if done by the church directly. On the other hand, their successes can be adopted into the regular program of the church and thus conserved. Complete control of experimentation or demonstration work is likely to destroy or prevent initiative, which is the soul of progress.

In adjusting problems between denominations in local communities a number of plans have been tried with greater or less success. One of the oldest is that of the "union" church. This is a type of organization in which the people of the local community, tiring of the uneconomic system of interdenominational competition, and without hope of uniting on any one of the local organizations represented, decide to separate from all and form themselves into an independent local organization.

No large denomination to-day is favorable [Pg 128] to the so-called "union" church; and all are opposed to the plan sometimes followed by rural industrial concerns of erecting a church building open to anyone who pretends to speak with authority about religious matters. The "union" church usually begins with enthusiasm, but because of lack of outside contacts, because of lack of continuity of program, because of lack of a broad missionary spirit, it is generally shortlived and gives way to some church with denominational affiliations. The "union" church without denominational affiliations should not be confused with the "community" church with denominational connection. It is the latter type that most religious organizations are now agreed is most desirable as the solution of the inexcusable overchurching now existing in many communities.

In these days of get-together movements denominational leaders should think clearly with reference to "federated" churches. A few of these have had a fairly long life. But their growth in the past fifteen years has not been such as to inspire confidence that they offer a satisfactory solution to the [Pg 129] overchurched situation. The "federated" church idea is not in harmony with a connectional polity nor with the principle of world democracy with centralization of administrative responsibility for carrying out democratically adopted plans implied in that polity. Local federation involves giving of full power of selection of pastors and of determination of policies to the local congregation. Whatever may be said about the occasional failures of the connectional system in finding suitable pastors, or in other ways, it is nevertheless true that this system has a vitality and efficiency that are now being recognized by many of the leading religious organizations. The polity of the "federated" church is congregational; and extreme congregationalism and connectionalism do not mix readily so far as polity is concerned. The growth of the one form involves the decline of the other. This is why the Methodist Episcopal Church, for example, has developed so little sympathy for the "federated" church idea.

Far different from this is allocation of responsibility for community leadership. This insures leadership to one denomination [Pg 130] or the other. Then the local congregations can work out their problems of adjustment as local conditions indicate is best. Usually some form of affiliation in worship and in sharing local expenses with continued separation of support of missionary and other benevolent enterprises has proven the most satisfactory method of local adjustment. By this method connectional interests are preserved and fixing of responsibility in each community assured.

With the vastly increased missionary resources made available by the missionary "drives" of the leading denominations there is positive danger of the problem of interdenominational adjustment being made still more serious. If the Home Mission Boards, through unwise use of mission funds for the purpose of assisting in competitive struggles, should precipitate retaliation by other denominations, a misuse of missionary funds would result that would not only dry up the sources of missionary support but bring Protestantism into lasting disgrace.

In working out a program of interdenominational adjustment the following plan has been tried with success on at least three [Pg 131] Methodist Episcopal Annual Conference districts:

1. A survey of the district and the preparation of a map showing the location of all churches, residences of all pastors, circuit systems, and whether churches are located in villages or the open country.

2. Separate lists are then made of cases of apparent competitive relations with each denomination.

3. Conferences are then called with the representatives of each denomination to consider the problems of competition between the Methodist Episcopal Church and the particular denomination with which the conference is called.

4. After tentative plans have been adopted representatives of both denominations visit the local field together, confer with the churches concerned, and arrive at some agreement as to adjustments to be made.

5. This method is followed with each denomination, separately, with which Methodism has competitive relations.

This plan has been tried with success in the State of Vermont, where Methodists, [Pg 132] Baptists, and Congregationalists had to cooperate or abandon the field; in the Portsmouth district, Ohio Conference, where the principal problems were with the Presbyterians, United Brethren, and Baptists; in Montana, where a conference was held to consider adjustments affecting an entire State; and in the Wooster District, North-East Ohio Conference, where adjustment of relationships is proceeding satisfactorily.

The results of this program already noticeable are:

1. The increase in salary of rural ministers made possible by uniting the financial resources of all religious forces in the community.

2. Saving of missionary money by eliminating duplication of missionary grants by competing denominations.

3. A marked increase in membership and church attendance.

4. A more vital relationship of the church to community welfare through unified action of all religious forces under the trained leadership of one pastor.

5. Resident pastorates to more communities through better distribution of pastoral [Pg 133] residences of the denominations concerned in adjustments made.

6. A more vital appeal to life service in rural work can now be made to young people who have objected to service in rural charges where efforts at community service have been handicapped and even nullified by the presence of competing religious organizations and pastors.

It is believed that the results obtained far outweigh the possible losses that may come through Methodists intrusting leadership in service to Presbyterians, Congregationalists, Baptists, or the reverse. The good work made possible by fixing responsibility for leadership to a given denomination in one community is destined by the force of example and imitation to compel similar progress in communities to which leadership responsibility has been assigned to other denominations.

A word of caution to ministers in charge of local fields is desirable in regard to settlement of interdenominational difficulties. The interests involved are so much larger than the local church that the initiative must be taken by the district superintendent, [Pg 134] always in the fullest consultation with the resident bishop, or the proper State, synodical, or other representative of the other denominations concerned. In a number of cases local initiative in this matter has resulted not only in defeating the end sought but has created embarrassing situations between the supervisory representatives of the denominations. If a local situation needs adjustment, the matter should be gone over fully with those responsible for church administration, and it is believed that in most cases such adjustment can be made satisfactorily. The experience of those in the Methodist Episcopal Church who have tried to bring about adjustments by the method suggested has been that in most cases other groups are ready to come to an agreement.

If other groups refuse to make adjustments, then the denomination making the advances has no other alternative than that of caring for its own obligations as adequately as possible and with every resource that can be made available. But no blame can attach to this policy after effort has been made to cooperate with other groups and these efforts have failed.

[Pg 135]

After communities have been allocated for leadership to one or another of the denominations, then the problem of a united program by all denominations remains to be solved. Unless this end is attained, then rural churches must continue to work largely alone, each in its own community without relation to the program of neighboring churches or communities. Unless there is coordination between the churches, then we shall continue to witness the spectacle of the three interdenominational branches of the church, the Sunday School Association, and the Christian Associations, each moving in its own self-chosen direction, each raising an independent budget, and each establishing county organizations without reference to the interests of the other; and none of the three doing anything to encourage the organization of county groups of the churches as such. The time has arrived when the church as such should take the lead in bringing about interdenominational cooperation for community service under its own auspices and in the most inclusive way.

For many reasons the county offers the best basis for this type of organization. It is [Pg 136] the most permanent political unit, next to the State or the incorporated town or city. Social progress finds the closest opportunity for cooperation with economic and political agencies in the county. The following proposal for a County Christian Association, supported out of the budgets of local cooperating churches, has been worked out:

Suggested Program for County Rural Christian Association or Federation of Churches [1]

- 1a. Proposal for County Christian Association or Church Federation.
    - o 1b. Board of Directors.
        - 1c. County Council chosen by each cooperating denomination on basis of membership.
        - 2c. Election or appointment of denominational representatives to be left to each denomination.
        - 3c. Selection of county secretary.
    - o 2b. Duties of county secretary.
        - 1c. Survey — Follow up what interchurch county office has done.
            - 1d. Location of all churches.
            - 2d. Residence of pastors.
            - 3d. Community boundaries.
        - 2c. Organize county religious movements as: [Pg 137]
            - 1d. Evangelistic drive.
            - 2d. Membership rally.
            - 3d. Go-to-church campaigns.
            - 4d. Religious worship in the home.
            - 5d. Common programs with reference to moral and spiritual problems.
            - 6d. Other religious movements.
        - 3c. Interchurch adjustments.
            - 1d. Act as secretary of Committee on Adjustments — provide office for interchurch activities.
            - 2d. Depository for interchurch religious information.

- 3d. Follow-up plans made as result of interchurch survey, including:
    - 1e. Encouragement of building parsonage and getting resident pastor in every community.
    - 2e. Getting a community church building in every community adequate to its needs.
    - 3e. Getting a community building under joint religious auspices where need exists for several houses of worship.
    - 4e. Clearing house for membership conservation.
    - 5e. Determination of parish boundaries.
    - 6e. Establishment of new work in communities where there is none.
- 4c. Social and recreational. [Pg 138]
    - 1d. County field days.
    - 2d. Cooperation in organizing boys' and girls' clubs in Sunday school or otherwise.
    - 4d. Direct social and recreational activities.
    - 5d. Assisting in selection and training leaders for church and community service.
- 5c. Religious education.
    - 1d. Recruiting membership campaigns.

- - - 2d. Perform all functions now expected of volunteer county Sunday school secretary.
        - 3d. Assist in analysis of Sunday school methods and organization in local churches in organizing for larger service.
        - 4d. Week-day religious instruction plans.
    - 6c. Social service activities to be encouraged:
        - 1d. County free library.
        - 2d. County hospital and nursing program.
        - 3d. Adequate provision for dependents, defectives, delinquents.
        - 4d. Securing desired State public service.
        - 5d. Health and sanitation campaign.
        - 6d. County Farm bureaus.
    - 7c. Cooperation with other agencies. In general, give moral support [Pg 139] to agencies doing effective work in the fields mentioned in (6c).
    - 8c. Act as bureau of advice with reference to appeals for charitable purposes.
    - 9c. Religious publicity.
  - 3b. Budget.
    - 1c. Estimated Salary of Secretary $3,000
      Travel 400
      Office rent 300
      Equipment 200
      Stenographer 750
      Publicity 40

      — — —

      $5,050

    - 2c. How to raise.

- 1d. Estimate amount that should come from each cooperating church. Ask each church to assume its share on a three-year guarantee.
- 2d. Make list of special givers who may become a private source.
- 3d. Communicate with respective missionary boards for aid in carrying balance of budget until such time as it can be brought to self-support.

[1] Prepared in Collaboration with C. J. Hewett, Garrett Biblical Institute, Evanston, Ill.

This form of organization has many advantages, among which are:

1. It coordinates all the religious forces [Pg 140] of Protestantism, for a common community service.

2. It insures ultimate permanent support by being financed out of the budgets of the cooperating churches instead of by a limited number of private givers of large funds.

3. The county organization develops its work through the churches, strengthening the program of the minister instead of developing independent organizations locally with volunteer leadership related to an "arm" of the church instead of directly to the church.

4. By organizing to do their own work in this way the churches obviate the necessity of private Christian agencies organizing with outside support to carry on interdenominational work.

If the churches of America do not rapidly work out plans of interdenominational cooperation in the development of their work, other agencies will enter the field and will receive popular financial support for doing those things in rural progress that are the legitimate task of the church and for which the church should receive support. Church people will supply the large part of the [Pg 141] funds for carrying on these activities through nonreligious agencies; and because of the narrowness of program the church will have chosen for itself many of the brightest and best minds, and consecrated hearts now found in our student groups in educational institutions will find their life's activities outside the church instead of within its ranks where they would prefer to be. This will be the misfortune of the church and she cannot clear herself of the wrong of depriving her young people of the opportunity of rendering a service to humanity within her own ranks and of forcing them to render that service through independent social agencies.

[Pg 142]

CHAPTER IX

THE CHURCH AND OTHER RURAL AGENCIES

Since the arousal of interest in rural welfare by the studies made by the Country Life Commission in 1908, probably no movement has made more rapid progress than that concerned with rural life. Studies of rural church conditions made by the Presbyterian Board of Home Missions and other agencies, of rural health by the National Public Health Service and by a number of the large philanthropic foundations, of educational conditions by the United States Bureau of Education, and of other problems by various agencies concerned, have revealed the more important conditions and have made possible the organization of programs for their amelioration. The conditions still further revealed by the problems incident to preparation for the World War and the facilities made possible by that preparation for mobilization of the forces for improvement [Pg 143] still further advanced the rural-life movement until now no other interest is occupying more public attention than this.

The list of agencies with programs of rural service on a national scale that have found representation in the National Council of Rural Social Service affiliated with the American Country Life Association will indicate the large number of groups now contributing to the advance of rural welfare. This list is as follows: National Grange, American Farm Bureau Federation, National Board of Farm Organizations, Farmers' Educational and Cooperative Union, American Home Economics Society, American Red Cross, Boy Scouts of America, Girl Scouts of America, Federal Council of Churches, National Catholic Welfare Council, Board of Home Missions of the Presbyterian Church in the United States of America, American Baptist Home Missionary Society, Board of Home Missions of the Methodist Episcopal Church, Young Men's Christian Association, Young Women's Christian Association, United States Department of Agriculture, States Relations Service; United States Department of [Pg 144] Agriculture, Office of Farm Management; United States Public Health Service, United States Bureau of Education, United States Department of Labor, Children's Bureau; National Organization for Public Health Nursing, National Child Labor Committee,

Child Health Organization of America, Russell Sage Foundation, National Tuberculosis Association, National Educational Association, Rural Department; American Library Association, National University Extension Association, National Child Health Council, Playground and Recreation Association of America, Community Service, Inc.

The above is a list of thirty-one different agencies that have a national definitely organized rural-service program. This list doubtless is incomplete and will be increased in the course of time.

The problem before us is to determine just what place the church should have in this formidable galaxy of agencies, and to consider what advantages and difficulties present themselves to the churches of America in functioning unitedly and successfully in doing their part in the entire movement.

[Pg 145]

It must be recognized that it is impossible for the church to assume leadership in all the interests represented now by various specialized agencies. It has been contended that the task of the church has been completed with reference to a number of these interests when it has encouraged their organization in a local way and has continued to give them its moral support so long as they render effectively the service for which they were intended. Rural interests are so complex that specialized groups are necessary to insure adequate attention to all the interests concerned.

It must also be recognized that until the two great branches of the Christian Church—Catholicism and Protestantism—learn to cooperate in their service to the community, the religious forces of America cannot present a united front in rendering the service that belongs peculiarly to them. It is assumed that the effort will be made by those responsible for community service in both branches of the church to work out this problem so that the church can do its part in the general movement.

The physical basis for organization of all [Pg 146] forces for service on a comprehensive plan is recognized to be the political units, county, State, and nation. The township is giving way gradually to the community as the more local unit of organization. In cases where community boundary lines do not coincide with county lines local adjustments will be made whereby the integrity of communities may be maintained within the organization of one or the other of the counties concerned.

The present movement is toward the appointment of county work secretaries on a salaried basis to administer the work of the respective interests concerned. Thus we have now developed wherever the spirit of the people has made it possible salaried County Y. M. C. A. officers, Y. W. C. A. officers, International Sunday School officers, Red Cross Chapters, Boy Scouts, Community Service, Inc., and so forth. There is no regularity or uniformity in the selection of the counties by the different agencies with reference to each other, but it appears that when one of the groups succeeds in getting a county office established, it is increasingly difficult for other agencies concerned in rural social service to gain a [Pg 147] foothold on a salaried basis. The agency that succeeds in gaining a foothold originally tends to incorporate into its activities the full program of social service. Theoretically all admit their readiness to turn over to other agencies the functions belonging to other groups as soon as they are ready to assume their proper duties, but practically the organization of an interest group county office delays indefinitely the organization of rural service on a proper basis.

The normal course of development is for the agency that is prepared to organize and finance a comprehensive rural program for a county should render this service; but it should at the same time use its influence to bring about at the earliest possible moment a county council of social agencies that will give unified control of the rural service program to all agencies that should have a voice in rural progress. If this policy is adhered to, there will be the heartiest support of the work of any agency that wishes to begin its work on a county basis in any section of the country.

The first impression that may come to one not familiar with the vastness of the organized [Pg 148] movement for rural welfare may be that a large number of agencies have undertaken rural service for their own sakes rather than for the sake of the community. This is not the case. It is recognized that rural organization for definite objectives should take the place of previous uncoordinated, haphazard opportunism in rural progress, and the present sporadic and unrelated movements toward organization are but the result of a very rapid development which has not yet found time to make the desired adjustment desired by all concerned. The National Council of Rural Social Agencies, the State Councils coming into existence, the County Councils and the community councils that have appeared here and there are but the beginnings of a well-ordered, economical and necessary coordination of rural social forces.

How is the church related to this movement? Repeated investigations have shown that the churches of America have within their membership by far the larger proportion of those whose public spirit registers itself in voluntary financial support of public enterprises. The "friendly citizen" is largely a myth. Those who build churches [Pg 149] at large personal sacrifice, and pay the bills in maintaining religious services are those whose names appear at the top of most subscriptions to benevolent enterprises. It was the Christian ministry and the church membership that made possible the Red Cross drives during the war, and the other financial campaigns for relief and other calls incident to the war. Thus history has continued to show the same condition so far as financial resources for public welfare support are concerned.

Since this is the case, it appears that the most natural method of initiating social service work on a voluntary basis is to expect the churches to take the lead. As has been pointed out, the church and the school are the two local institutions that have salaried officials to care for their public service. Other agencies, with the possible exception of public health nursing service, will probably not in the near future be able to secure financial support for full-time salaried local officials. The nearest they can approach to such salaried service is the county official who must depend for local service upon trained volunteer help. This condition puts [Pg 150] upon the church an additional responsibility because through the organization of a county religious organization outlined in the preceding chapter it can not only mobilize local support for such work on a permanent basis most effectively, but it can also provide the salaried local leadership for carrying out a well-organized community service program. Moreover, in harmony with principles presented in an earlier chapter, the church as a conservative institution is one of the permanent organizations that in the last analysis must be expected to take over and insure permanence to well-tried advances in community organization and service. If this thesis is admitted, then it logically follows that all who are interested in rural progress should encourage the organization of the religious forces on a comprehensive basis to insure the perpetuation of the work now being inaugurated by a large number of private agencies.

When it is found that the interests of other organizations conflict with the program of the church, the interests of the American public will give the preference in support to the church, or to the tax-supported [Pg 151] institution. In the long run much of the work now being done by private organizations of various sorts will be inherited either by the church or by the state; and it is not only the opportunity but the obligation of the church to prepare itself as rapidly as possible for conserving these newer activities by financing county and State and national organizations for coordination of religious forces for community service. If county offices for coordination of religious forces were now in existence, the churches could provide facilities through which much of the work now being developed by other agencies could be carried on. And thus the church could render a much-needed service to the entire rural-life movement.

[Pg 152]

CHAPTER X

MISSIONARY PROGRAMS AND RURAL COMMUNITY SERVICE

Long years of experience in foreign missionary service has vitally affected the methods of carrying the gospel of Christian living to those who have not yet come under the influence of the Christ. Here the demonstration method of what Christianity means in terms of increased human welfare has done far more to spread the gospel than simply preaching to people. The freeing of the millions now living under the control of other forms of religious belief by introduction of schools, together with the message of health and better moral ideals through the practice of Christian living, has done more to spread Christianity than all the efforts of attempting to build a Christian spirit into a civilization not suited to it nor prepared for it.

The missionary agencies in the home [Pg 153] fields have learned from the experience in the foreign fields, and now the programs of home missionary boards are characterized by their large emphasis upon the social gospel. The revival of interest in religious life in this country coincident with the recognition of its vital significance in sound social organization has come so rapidly and popular support has been so liberal that grave danger exists lest the funds made available should be used unintentionally in ways that tend to defeat the purpose of the gift. The church, in its benevolent program, should take advantage of the lessons learned by private philanthropic agencies in dealing with problems of reclamation of the unfortunate or of stimulating to a larger life.

Many of the efforts at social progress fail because of lack of clear statement of objectives. So far as the rural work is concerned, the following are presented as necessary objectives, if the rural church is to succeed in measuring up to its task. It is believed that funds of the church can be used safely and wisely in their attainment.

1. Strengthen the weak places in rural church work in harmony with principles of [Pg 154] interdenominational ethics and well-established principles of benevolent assistance.

2. Increase effectiveness of rural ministry by training ministry now in service in modern methods of church work and by recruiting and training a new ministry in sympathy with rural life and devoted to its improvement.

3. Organize rural church work so that every rural family will have definitely assigned pastoral care.

4. Adjust interdenominational relationships so that the ideal of but one resident pastor and one church to each community may be realized.

5. Provide means of interdenominational cooperation so that rural religious forces may work together in dealing with common problems of rural social and religious progress.

6. Organize rural work so that it may have due consideration in the general policies of religious organizations.

7. All the above are preliminary to the one great object, from the social point of view, namely, that of making it possible for the rural church and the rural minister to [Pg 155] function most effectively in bringing more abundant life in the best sense to rural people.

After religious forces are organized so that they can present a united front in the attack on the great social problems of rural life, then the individual churches and all churches together can undertake to meet the challenge outlined in earlier chapters of this text and also well presented in much of the recent literature on the subject. But effective organization must precede most effective and permanent service.

Certain principles have been the guiding influence in the program on which the rural department of at least one of the leading denominations has been working. For those who come to positions of administrative responsibility from time to time without having been under the necessity of acquainting themselves with the principles that should guide in the safe expenditure of funds for maintenance of pastors, these are given here:

1. Principles of interdenominational ethics should be observed in making grants of missionary funds to local pastors. It is to [Pg 156] be feared that too often funds have been used to sustain a local

work in the presence of another denomination when efforts at interdenominational adjustment would have relieved the situation by removing the necessity, namely, that of division of local resources by competing religious forces.

2. Owing to the unusual problems presented on charges asking for missionary aid only the ablest ministers should be assigned to such points. They should be supported according to their needs through missionary aid, and their acceptance of difficult work should enhance rather than lessen their standing in the church.

3. Rigid avoidance of use of missionary funds for purposes of charity, or for making appointments easier. The charge, not the minister, is the objective.

4. Centralization of effort on a few places instead of dissipation of funds in providing inefficient service in many places.

5. Gradual but certain withdrawal of support from national or State boards in order to avoid pauperizing communities by relieving them of their local financial responsibilities.

[Pg 157]

As one of the most serious problems connected with rural missionary service is that of interdenominational complications, an effort has been made to work out certain principles that may be observed by all religious organizations carrying out a rural program. At the annual meeting of the Home Missions Council in 1914 a statement of principles was adopted. In 1919 the rural fields committee of the Home Missions Council undertook the revision of these principles in the light of later experience and adopted the revision as a committee report. Because this document represents the best judgment of those in the various denominations concerned with rural work it is presented herewith as a desirable basis on which grants of funds may be safely made. The statement is presented in full:

Persuaded of the urgent need of some comprehensive and united plan for the evangelization of our country and for closer cooperation to make such plans effective, the Home Missions Council proposes for the consideration of its constituent societies the following principles of comity. It is to be distinctly understood, however, that no ecclesiastical authority of any kind is implied [Pg 158] except as ecclesiastical bodies shall adopt these policies as their own. They have only the moral force of the consent of the parties desiring to see them become effective.

First. As to the occupancy of new fields. The frequently suggested plan for the entering of new territory is to divide it among the various denominations, holding each body responsible for the proper working of its field.

1. In the judgment of this Council this course of procedure would seem to be impracticable. But a sensitive regard not only for the rights but for the sentiments of sister bodies of Christian people is demanded by every consideration of righteousness as well as fraternity.
2. In districts or in places already occupied by any denomination new work should be undertaken by any other body only after fraternal conference between the official representatives of the missionary organizations embracing those localities.
3. Occupancy of the field shall be determined by at least the following characteristics:
     1. The establishment of a regularly organized church.

        The establishing of a Sunday school shall not be deemed sufficient to meet the terms of this definition.
     2. The appointment of a pastor who shall [Pg 159] be expected to hold services in the community at least once every two weeks.
     3. The provision of church building and equipment within a reasonable time adequate to the needs of the community at its present stage of development.

The occupation of a field by any denomination after conference and agreement shall give to that denomination the right to the field and the responsibility for its Christian culture until such changes in population shall make it desirable that it be shared with one or more other denominations.

94

If the above conference shall fail to reach agreement, it shall be the privilege of the aggrieved party to make appeal to its respective board or society, which board or society shall confer with the sister board or society concerned, and these boards may then request the superintendents of the denominations concerned for the field in question to make personal investigation and to report their findings to their respective boards. If they agree, the boards shall take action in accordance therewith. If they disagree, the matter shall be referred to the boards for such action as their wisdom may determine, which action shall be communicated to the churches concerned with whatever ecclesiastical or moral force their decision may command.

Second. In communities already occupied by two or more denominations, in case any church or mission station shall consider itself aggrieved [Pg 160] in its relations to sister churches, the course of procedure outlined in Section I shall likewise be followed.

There shall be friendly conference in the spirit of the Great Head of the church and recourse be had, when necessary, to the local or national missionary authorities, whose findings properly communicated shall have behind them the moral force of this Council.

Where any denomination occupies a district by groupings of mission stations under one missionary the same principles shall apply and the same method of adjusting differences shall be followed.

Third. "Overchurched Communities." Not infrequently the promise of new towns fails of fulfillment, with the result that there are more church organizations than in any economic view should be maintained—at least out of missionary funds. In many sections of the country also, because of the marked shift of population from agricultural communities to urban centers, overchurching has weakened all denominations to the point where missionary effort is necessary to restore again a wholesome religious life. Regardless of the cause of overchurching, whether from the undue optimism of the newer sections of the country or changed conditions in the older, or other conditions, the problem of overchurching must be dealt with in the true spirit of comity and cooperation for the sake of the common good.

1. The principle should be established that one [Pg 161] Protestant church is adequate for each community of less than 1,500 inhabitants; and that efforts should be made to bring about interdenominational readjustment to this end in all sections of the country where economic and social conditions have become sufficiently established to make improbable any marked or rapid increase in population within a short time.
2. In communities of over 1,500 inhabitants there should not be more than one Protestant church to every 1,000 population.
3. In communities of over 1,500 inhabitants and of less than 5,000, plans should be worked out whereby the different denominations concerned shall cooperate in providing adequate building and equipment for community service. Such building should be strategically located and should be controlled by a governing board made up of representatives, the number of whom from each denomination shall be determined by the *constituency* of that denomination in its proportion to the total Protestant or cooperating population. The rules for the control of the activities of such cooperative community service should respect the standards of the respective denominations. The support of such community service should be apportioned to the respective denominations concerned to [Pg 162] be raised in their respective budgets in proportion to their respective representation on the governing board.
4. It shall be the duty of the denomination to which responsibility shall have been allocated to provide the best-trained leadership and the best service of which it is capable out of consideration to the other denominations that have intrusted the spiritual welfare of their membership to this group.
5. In determining what denomination has prime responsibility in a given community of under 1,500 inhabitants the following shall be considered.
    1. Present resident membership and constituency. The organization having the largest bona fide membership and constituency should be consid-

ered as having prime responsibility, from this point of view.

2. The residence of the pastor. In general, the pastor's residence should be given larger weight than membership unless the denomination having prime responsibility according to (1) stands ready to provide a pastor's residence in the community where this denomination has prime responsibility from the point of view of membership.

3. The location of the church building. The [Pg 163] denomination that has a building located in a village center should be given precedence over the denomination that has its headquarters in the open country near a village. The building of the village church should be suitably located for adequate community service; that is, near the center of the village.

4. As between the village and the open country church, the village church should be given prime consideration in putting on an aggressive community program.

5. No missionary or "sustentation" support should be given by any cooperating denomination to a pastor in an overchurched community nor to a "circuit" involving interdenominational competition until after an adjustment is made either by reorganization of the circuit or an agreement has been reached by the missionary and administrative bodies of the respective denominations concerned as to an allocation of such missionary responsibility.

6. Church extension aid should not be given toward the rebuilding of churches in these communities until after allocation of responsibility has been effected.

7. If after due effort to secure satisfactory adjustment of relationships according to the plans suggested in First above, [Pg 164] and by such further arbitration or other means as may be adopted by the Home Missions Council or its constituent bodies,

then the denomination seeking such adjustment shall be at liberty to develop its own work as it may see fit, standing ready, however, to make agreement with competing bodies whenever they wish to renew negotiations.

8. In the interests of the Kingdom, after missionary responsibility has been allocated, efforts at unifying local religious organizations may take the form of federation, assimilation, affiliation, or such other mode as may be determined on by the local churches concerned.

9. Plans should also be worked out whereby the religious forms of the different groups may be respected; that is, that membership in the remaining religious organization may be obtained by fulfilling the obligations of the cooperating body with which the persons belonging to the withdrawing organization would naturally affiliate.

10. It is understood that nothing in this proposed set of principles implies that withdrawal from given fields shall be forced. It is only intended to provide a plan whereby all forces both local and general shall be united as rapidly as [Pg 165] possible in the attainment of the desired end, namely, that of unifying Christian service in given communities.

11. In determining the limits of communities to which this plan shall apply the Federal Census Bureau designation of communities of 2,500 and under as rural shall be adopted except as noted in paragraph 5c.

Fourth. Inasmuch as many of the constituent bodies of this Council are already by official action committed to the principles of comity which we advocate, it would seem reasonable to hope that at least gradually these principles would find realization along some such lines as here proposed.

It is manifest, of course, that no plan of procedure can be expected to cover all cases or to be of universal applicability. We are glad to record that in some States there are Interchurch Federations to which local comity matters would naturally be referred. For other cases this Council proposes the erection of an Interdenominational Commission, to which any matter of comity not otherwise provided for may be referred by mutual agreement of the parties at interest. One representative of each of the bodies having membership in the Home Missions Council shall constitute this commission. When any case calling for adjudication shall rise, which case shall previously have had the consideration of any one or more of the constituent bodies of the Home Missions [Pg 166] Council, it shall be referred to a Committee of Three chosen from this committee and acceptable to both parties. The decision of this committee shall have no ecclesiastical force, but its utterance shall be regarded as voicing the united judgment of the Home Missions Council and so far forth shall be binding on its constituent bodies.

It is recognized that these principles do not receive the most enthusiastic support of church leaders who are thinking in terms of denominational progress instead of community welfare. But this lack of support is an evidence of their value instead of a criticism. Denominational interests must be sacrificed for the sake of the advancement of the entire cause when the two come into conflict. There is reason to hope that not only Protestants but also Catholics and Protestants can come to cooperate on programs of community service, thus overcoming forever the vital objection to religious leadership now made that because of fundamental differences in belief the two great branches of the church cannot render an organized community service.

The relations of the benevolent boards of the several denominations to other church [Pg 167] organizations are such that but little can be said concerning methods of relating missionary work to the larger program of community service. In each case where projects for missionary aid are presented effort should be made to see that local conditions are made such that the pastor can render the best service. It must be recognized that the application for outside aid is in itself an admission of local weakness. The people are poor, or indifferent to the type of service to which they have been accustomed. There has been unforeseen disaster, as the destruction of church property by fire or in some other way. Sudden movements of population have temporarily weakened the support of the church and new resources have not yet been developed. Circuit systems must be broken up so that people will be willing to support full-time resident pastors with efficient programs for service. Customs of expecting the pastor to make his living in outside work and attending to religious service as a side issue must be overcome. The pastor's residence may be in such condition that families cannot be sacrificed for the sake of missionary communities and residences [Pg 168] must be supplied by liberal outside aid as the preliminary to effective service. Church buildings are inadequate, and the trained minister must be given every assurance that aid will be rendered in bringing physical equipment up to par. In each case the problems that present themselves must be met. The demands of any one charge do not compare with the demands of any other. And methods must be adapted to meet the specific needs of each charge. These are matters that must be left to those responsible for administration of missionary funds.

When the religious forces of America learn their problems so that a long-time organized program of religious advance can be worked out, when they learn to cooperate in carrying out this program, then the haphazard, wasteful, competitive missionary program that has characterized rural religious work in the past will disappear and we shall see one of the most marked advances in religious welfare the world has ever known.

[Pg 169]

CHAPTER XI

SUMMARY AND CONCLUSION

In the preceding chapters the effort has been made to outline some of the conditions and principles involved in organizing the rural church for community service. The field has been limited by distinguishing between that type of service which has to do with man's relation to his Maker and that which has to do with his relations to his fellow man. The latter service has been chosen as the field for the present discussion, and the effort has been made to keep within the field, regardless of the desirability of discussion of the other phases of the work of the rural church. The field itself both as to size of community and the scope of the entire field has received attention. An attempt has been made to present the philosophic basis justifying the church in giving large attention to community service. Some of the more general aspects of rural life demanding attention on the part of the church [Pg 170] have been discussed and the reasons for assuming that certain phases of rural social activity properly belong to the church rather than to other agencies have been presented to the reader.

The problems of adjustment between religious denominations as such and between the parent religious organizations and so-called "arms" of the church have been outlined and methods of adjustment suggested. The relation of all religious forces to other rural life agencies has received some attention; and, finally, the missionary program of the church as the agency for strengthening the weak and of advancing the general cause of conquest of all life with principles of Christian living was discussed. It is hoped that the principles presented will at least be given careful consideration, and if they are not accepted in full, that they will at least provoke discussion that will eventually lead to some form of organization that will more nearly meet the demands of the time than the present unorganized, unrelated sectarian and other efforts that paralyze and discourage those responsible for service in the local as well as in more general fields of [Pg 171] Christian work. If this object can be accomplished, the effort to point the direction organization should take will not have been in vain.